Table of contents

Introduction 6

Chapter 1 Heart of the Kitchen – Foundations First 8

    Kitchen Tools Every Cook Needs 9

    Pantry Staples: Your Culinary Toolkit 11

    Spices & Herbs: Flavor Building Blocks 13

    Prep Like a Pro: Cutting, Chopping, and Storing 15

Chapter 2 Morning Fuel – Breakfast to Power Your Day ... 17

    Quick & Healthy Breakfasts 18

    Brunch Classics Reinvented 20

    Smoothies, Bowls & Energy Boosters 21

    Make-Ahead Morning Meals 23

Chapter 3 Bites & Nibbles – Snacks & Starters That 26

    Dips & Spreads with a Kick 27

    Finger Foods for Every Occasion 29

    Light Bites with Big Flavor 31

    Savory Pastries & Mini Sandwiches 33

Chapter 4 Comfort in a Bowl – Soups & Stews 35

    Hearty Stews for Chilly Nights 36

Recipe: This Clearly Indicates A Collection Of Culinary Instructions

Clear Soups & Broths for Light Days 37

Global Soup Delights 39

Sides & Breads That Pair Perfectly 41

Chapter 5 Fresh & Flavorful – Salads Beyond the Basics... 44

Green Goodness: Leafy Salads 45

Grain Bowls & Hearty Bases 47

Protein-Packed Salad Meals 48

Dressings, Toppings & Crunch 51

Chapter 6 Weeknight Wonders – Easy Main Courses 53

One-Pot and One-Pan Recipes 54

Quick Stove-Top Favorites 56

30-Minute Meals 58

Mix & Match Dinner Combos 59

Chapter 7 From the Oven – Bakes, Roasts & Gratins 62

Casseroles & Comfort Bakes 63

Roasted Vegetables & Sides 65

Baked Pasta & Stuffed Dishes 66

Sheet Pan Magic 68

Chapter 8 Around the World on a Plate – Global 71

Asian Delights: Stir-Fries & Dumplings 72

Mediterranean Magic: Mezze & Mains 74

    Latin Flavors: Tacos, Rice, and Beans 75

    European Comforts: Pastas & Pies..77

Chapter 9 Sweet Treats – Desserts to Crave 80

    Cakes, Cupcakes & Loaves 81

    Pies, Tarts & Crisps..83

    Cookies & No-Bake Treats 85

    Fruity Endings & Light Options..87

Chapter 10 Plant-Powered Plates – Vegetarian & Veg 89

    Vibrant Veggie Mains 90

    Meatless Protein Options...92

    Dairy-Free Sauces & Substitutes...94

    Creative Vegan Desserts..96

Chapter 11 Feasts & Gatherings – Cooking for a Crowd 99

    Festive Appetizers & Starters..100

    Shareable Mains & Platters 102

    Side Dishes to Impress 104

    Sweet Celebrations 106

Chapter 12 Tips, Variations & Your Culinary Space 109

    Ingredient Swaps & Smart Substitutions....................................110

    Plating & Presentation Tips...112

    Storing, Freezing, and Reheating 114

Recipe Pages for Your Own Creations 116
Conclusion **118**

Introduction

Welcome to Recipe: This Clearly Indicates a Collection of Culinary Instructions — a cookbook crafted not only to teach but to inspire. Whether you're a beginner learning to boil an egg or a home cook seeking new flavor adventures, this book is your trusted companion on a journey through the art and joy of cooking.

In today's fast-paced world, preparing a meal can feel like a task rather than a pleasure. Yet, the kitchen remains one of the few places where creativity, nourishment, and connection all meet. With a pinch of patience and a dash of curiosity, even the simplest ingredients can transform into something extraordinary. This book is built on that belief — that cooking is not just about feeding the body but also about fueling the soul.

Each chapter in this book focuses on a different aspect of cooking — from energizing breakfasts and wholesome weeknight dinners to globally inspired dishes and sweet indulgences. You'll also find helpful tips on how to set up your kitchen, store ingredients efficiently, and plate your dishes like a pro. With each recipe, we aim to simplify steps without compromising on flavor, so that cooking remains accessible, fun, and rewarding.

We've also included sections for vegetarian and vegan options, recipes for special gatherings, and even a space at the end of the book for your own creations — because your kitchen journey should always reflect your personal taste, family traditions, and culinary dreams.

This isn't just a recipe book. It's a toolkit for everyday moments, from the solo dinner after a long day to the joyful chaos of a family feast. It's about discovering the pleasure in trying something new, the comfort of mastering a favorite dish, and the confidence that comes from knowing you can make something delicious with your own two hands.

So, tie on your apron, preheat that oven, and get ready to stir up something wonderful. Because with the right recipe, anything is possible.

Chapter 1
Heart of the Kitchen – Foundations First

Before you whisk, stir, chop, or sauté, you need to understand the soul of every dish — your kitchen. This chapter is where your culinary journey truly begins, because no matter how exquisite a recipe may be, it's only as successful as the foundation behind it. The kitchen is not just a room filled with appliances and cookware — it is a creative space where flavors are born, traditions are kept alive, and stories are told through food.

Start by knowing your tools. From sharp chef's knives to sturdy cutting boards, measuring spoons to cast-iron skillets, each item plays a specific role in your cooking success. Learning which tools are essential (and which are optional) will save you both time and stress. Next, explore your pantry. Stocking up on staple ingredients such as oils, spices, grains, and condiments gives you the flexibility to whip up a variety of meals with minimal planning.

Organization is also key. A clean, well-arranged kitchen allows you to move with ease and focus on flavor rather than fumbling through cluttered drawers. This chapter will guide you through setting up an efficient, welcoming cooking environment — one where inspiration comes easily, and every meal feels like an act of care.

Because when the heart of the kitchen beats strong, every recipe that follows comes to life with confidence and joy.

Kitchen Tools Every Cook Needs

Walking into a well-stocked kitchen is like stepping into a painter's studio — every tool has a purpose, and every item contributes to a masterpiece in the making. For any cook, whether you're a seasoned pro or just starting out, having the right kitchen tools is essential. They not only make your work easier but also help improve the quality, efficiency, and consistency of your meals. While kitchen gadgets can seem endless, this guide focuses on the core tools every cook should have to build a reliable and functional foundation.

At the top of the list is a quality chef's knife. It's the one tool you'll reach for more than any other, and it's worth investing in a knife that feels balanced and sharp in your hand. A good chef's knife can handle slicing, chopping, dicing, and even delicate tasks like mincing herbs or trimming meat. Pair it with a sturdy cutting board — preferably wooden or BPA-free plastic — to give yourself a safe and stable surface for prep work. Remember, the better your prep tools, the more confident and efficient you'll feel while cooking.

Measuring cups and spoons are non-negotiables, especially for baking, where precision is key. Even if you prefer to cook by feel, having a reliable set on hand helps when following new recipes or replicating dishes. Dry measuring cups for flour, sugar, and other solids, and liquid measuring cups with easy-to-read markers for oils, broths, and milk — both are vital for any recipe arsenal.

Next up is a set of mixing bowls in varying sizes. These are your go-to for whisking, tossing salads, marinating meats, or simply keeping prepped ingredients organized. Stainless steel, glass, or BPA-free plastic options are durable and versatile, and stackable sets help save space. You'll also benefit from having a variety of utensils: a spatula for scraping and folding, wooden spoons for stirring without scratching, a ladle for soups and stews, and a whisk for blending sauces and batters.

A reliable non-stick skillet and a heavy-bottomed stainless steel or cast-iron pan will cover most of your stovetop needs. These are perfect for sautéing vegetables, searing proteins, and even making quick one-pan meals. Add a medium-sized saucepan and a large stockpot to the mix for boiling pasta, simmering soups, or preparing grains. If you're into baking or roasting, a rimmed sheet pan, a baking dish (like a 9x13 casserole pan), and a wire cooling rack are must-haves.

Let's not forget the small but mighty tools that make a big impact — a microplane for zesting citrus and grating cheese, tongs for flipping and serving, a can opener that actually works, and a vegetable peeler that glides smoothly. A colander or mesh strainer is also essential for draining pasta, rinsing beans, or washing produce. And for those who love efficiency, a food processor, blender, or immersion blender can save a lot of time and effort while expanding your cooking capabilities.

Staying organized is just as important as having the right gear. A drawer organizer for your utensils, a magnetic strip or knife block for storing blades safely, and labeled containers for dry goods or leftovers help maintain a clean, efficient workspace. Having everything within reach means fewer interruptions, less stress, and a more enjoyable cooking experience.

In the end, building your kitchen tool kit doesn't have to be overwhelming or expensive. Start with the basics, invest in quality where it matters most, and expand gradually as you grow more confident in your cooking. With the right tools at your fingertips, the kitchen becomes not just a place to cook, but a space to create, experiment, and connect with the food you love.

Pantry Staples: Your Culinary Toolkit

A well-stocked pantry is the secret weapon of every great cook. It's not just a place to store dry goods — it's your culinary toolkit, your flavor arsenal, and your safety net on nights when the fridge is bare. With the right pantry staples, you can whip up a meal in minutes, elevate simple ingredients, and avoid unnecessary last-minute trips to the grocery store. The beauty of pantry staples lies in their versatility. These are ingredients that don't spoil quickly, have endless applications, and form the foundation of countless recipes across all cuisines.

Let's begin with the essentials: grains and starches. Rice is a must-have — whether it's long-grain basmati, short-grain sushi rice, or hearty brown rice. Each type offers a different texture and flavor and can serve as the base for stir-fries, stews, curries, and even salads. Pasta, in its many shapes and sizes, is another kitchen hero. It cooks quickly, stores easily, and pairs with everything from olive oil and garlic to rich tomato sauces and creamy cheese blends. Don't overlook other shelf-stable grains like quinoa, couscous, oats, and bulgur, which are great for breakfast bowls, side dishes, or plant-based meals.

Canned goods are the backbone of pantry magic. Canned beans — such as chickpeas, black beans, and kidney beans — offer protein and fiber in a ready-to-use form. They're ideal for soups, salads, dips, or quick skillet meals. Stock up on canned tomatoes too, whether whole, crushed, diced, or in paste form. They're the foundation of many sauces, stews, and braises. Tuna, salmon, or sardines also make a strong case as pantry MVPs — perfect for sandwiches, pastas, or snacks when protein is needed in a pinch.

Next, we move to oils, vinegars, and condiments. A high-quality olive oil is a must for dressings, drizzling, and sautéing. Vegetable or canola oil works well for high-heat cooking, and sesame oil adds a nutty depth to Asian-inspired dishes. Vinegars are just as important — white vinegar for pickling, apple cider for tangy dressings, balsamic for bold marinades, and rice vinegar for light, balanced acidity. Add soy sauce, hot sauce, mustard, mayonnaise, and a few jars of your favorite chutneys or jams to instantly enhance flavor and variety.

Spices and dried herbs are where your pantry becomes truly personal. Start with the basics: salt and pepper, garlic and onion powder, paprika, cumin, chili flakes, and cinnamon. These alone can add warmth and complexity to a wide range of dishes. Expand your collection based on your preferences — maybe you love Indian curries, Mediterranean roasts, or Mexican street food. Keep your spices fresh by storing them in airtight containers away from direct heat or sunlight.

Don't forget baking essentials, even if you don't consider yourself a baker. All-purpose flour, baking soda, baking powder, sugar, brown sugar, honey, and yeast open the door to homemade breads, cakes, sauces, and even savory coatings and thickeners. Nuts, seeds, and dried fruits also pull double duty — adding texture to salads, sweetness to baking, or protein to snacks.

Lastly, your pantry should reflect your style and lifestyle. If you love smoothies, keep shelf-stable nut butters and protein powders on hand. If you're plant-based, dried lentils, nutritional yeast, and coconut milk are excellent additions. If you meal prep, consider including jarred sauces, grain blends, or vacuum-packed cooked lentils and beans for convenience.

A stocked pantry means freedom in the kitchen. It gives you the confidence to experiment, improvise, and nourish yourself and others without starting from scratch every time. So treat your pantry like your personal toolbox — keep it organized, refresh it often, and fill it with ingredients that spark creativity and support your everyday cooking adventures.

Spices & Herbs: Flavor Building Blocks

When it comes to cooking, spices and herbs are your secret allies — the subtle alchemists that transform ordinary ingredients into extraordinary dishes. They're the flavor building blocks that turn bland into bold, simple into sensational. With just a pinch, sprinkle, or dash, you can transport a dish across continents, awaken the senses, and infuse personality into every bite. Whether dried or fresh, whole or ground, spices and herbs are what give your food depth, complexity, and soul.

Spices come from seeds, bark, roots, and fruits of plants, and they often bring heat, warmth, or intense aromatic notes to a dish. Think of cinnamon's sweet spice in baked goods or cumin's smoky richness in curries and stews. Herbs, on the other hand, are the leafy parts of plants — like basil, parsley, thyme, and cilantro — and they tend to add freshness, brightness, or subtle green undertones. Used thoughtfully, they create balance and harmony in any recipe.

The key to mastering spices and herbs lies in understanding not only their flavors, but also how and when to use them. Some spices, like whole cloves, cardamom pods, or bay leaves, benefit from long cooking times to release their oils and mellow their intensity. Others, like paprika or turmeric, can burn easily and should be added with care. Fresh herbs like parsley and basil are often best added at the end of cooking to preserve their bright flavor and color, while hardy ones like rosemary and thyme can be cooked longer without losing potency.

Stocking a small but versatile collection of spices is a great start. Begin with salt and black pepper, then expand to garlic powder, onion powder, paprika, chili flakes, cumin, coriander, turmeric, cinnamon, and nutmeg. These can carry you through countless dishes, from roasted vegetables and soups to sauces and marinades. As your confidence grows, you can explore spice blends like curry powder, garam masala, Italian seasoning, or za'atar — each one offering a new world of flavor in a single jar.

When it comes to herbs, having a few dried options on hand — such as oregano, thyme, and dill — is always helpful. But nothing beats the vibrancy of fresh herbs. Keeping a small pot of basil or mint on the windowsill can be a game-changer, adding a fresh touch to everything from salads and pasta to teas and desserts.

Storing spices and herbs properly is essential to maintaining their flavor. Keep them in a cool, dark place away from heat and moisture, preferably in airtight containers. If your spices have lost their aroma or punch, it's probably time for a refresh — even the best spice can't save a dish if it's past its prime. For fresh herbs, wrapping them in a slightly damp paper towel and placing them in the fridge (or in a jar of water like a bouquet) can extend their life for several days.

Using spices and herbs well is a skill that develops with time and experimentation. Don't be afraid to trust your nose, taste as you go, and play with combinations. You'll quickly discover what you love, what enhances certain ingredients, and what makes your food uniquely yours.

At the heart of every memorable meal is flavor — and at the heart of flavor are the spices and herbs that bring it to life. Once you begin to use them with intention and curiosity, you'll find they're not just additions to a recipe — they're the essence of great cooking.

Prep Like a Pro: Cutting, Chopping, and Storing

In the rhythm of the kitchen, prep work is the heartbeat. It's the quiet but essential art that makes cooking smoother, faster, and infinitely more enjoyable. When you prep like a pro — with thoughtful chopping, efficient cutting, and smart storage — you give yourself the gift of ease and readiness. It's not just about slicing vegetables or portioning meat. It's about setting yourself up for culinary success before the heat even hits the pan.

Mastering knife skills is one of the first steps toward confidence in the kitchen. A sharp, well-balanced chef's knife can transform your experience, making every cut clean and precise. Learning the basic cutting techniques — like chopping, mincing, dicing, slicing, and julienning — can save you time and ensure even cooking. When ingredients are cut consistently, they cook consistently, leading to better texture and flavor. For example, evenly diced onions will caramelize more uniformly, and vegetables sliced to the same thickness will roast without some burning while others remain undercooked.

There's also a rhythm to prepping that's both efficient and satisfying. Line up your ingredients, group your tasks, and work in batches. Cut all your onions at once, then move on to garlic, then to carrots — instead of switching back and forth. Not only does this method save time, but it also reduces the number of tools you use and keeps your cutting board clean and organized.

Proper storage is the next part of the prep equation. Once you've chopped and portioned your ingredients, storing them the right way can extend freshness and save effort later. Airtight containers are essential — clear ones are best so you can see what's inside at a glance. Use them for chopped vegetables, pre-measured spices, marinated proteins, or portioned grains. Zip-top bags, silicone pouches, or mason jars also come in handy for space-saving storage, whether you're working with dry ingredients or prepped produce.

Labeling is a small step with a big payoff. Mark your containers with the date and contents so nothing gets forgotten in the fridge or freezer. For prepped fruits and vegetables, consider adding a paper towel at the bottom of the container to absorb moisture and help keep things crisp. And don't overlook freezing — it's a prepper's best friend. From diced onions and bell peppers to chopped herbs frozen in olive oil, freezing makes it easy to grab exactly what you need for cooking on busy days.

Another underrated aspect of prepping is building your mise en place — the practice of having everything measured, chopped, and ready before you start cooking. It's a technique used by professional chefs for good reason. When your ingredients are prepped and within reach, you can cook more mindfully, avoid burning anything while multitasking, and keep your space cleaner. It also helps eliminate last-minute surprises like missing ingredients or not having something chopped in time.

In essence, prepping like a pro is about planning, precision, and flow. It's a quiet discipline that turns chaos into calm, guesswork into intuition, and basic cooking into an experience of control and creativity. Whether you're preparing meals for the week or just trying to get dinner on the table without stress, a strong prep game turns your kitchen into a place of empowerment — where meals come together with intention, ease, and a little bit of culinary magic.

Chapter 2
Morning Fuel – Breakfast to Power Your Day

They say breakfast is the most important meal of the day — and for good reason. It sets the tone, fuels your energy, and jumpstarts both your metabolism and mood. In this chapter, we dive into the vibrant and nourishing world of breakfast, where simplicity meets satisfaction and every bite prepares you to take on the day ahead.

Whether you're someone who craves a hearty, hot meal first thing in the morning or prefers something light and on-the-go, this chapter offers a wide variety of breakfast recipes to suit every lifestyle. From protein-rich scrambles and wholesome overnight oats to smoothie bowls, muffins, and quick breakfast wraps — you'll discover both classic comforts and modern twists designed to energize and excite.

But breakfast is more than just food; it's a ritual. The aroma of coffee brewing, the soft sizzle of eggs in a pan, the gentle light of early morning — all these moments come together to create a peaceful beginning. That's why we also include tips for preparing ahead, so your mornings can feel calm, not rushed.

Whether you're cooking for yourself or for the whole family, these recipes are created with both nourishment and ease in mind.

With the right ingredients and a little planning, every day can begin with flavor, freshness, and the power of a good meal.

Quick & Healthy Breakfasts

Mornings can be chaotic — alarms ringing, kids rushing, meetings looming — and in all that bustle, breakfast often takes a back seat. But the first meal of the day doesn't have to be elaborate or time-consuming to be nourishing. Quick and healthy breakfasts are all about striking a balance between convenience and nutrition, ensuring that you fuel your body without adding stress to your morning routine. With a few smart strategies and go-to recipes, you can transform breakfast from an afterthought into a moment of calm, comfort, and care.

The key to success starts with ingredients that are both versatile and nutritious. Think whole grains, eggs, fruits, nuts, yogurt, seeds, and vegetables — all of which offer a powerful mix of fiber, protein, and essential nutrients. These ingredients form the backbone of countless quick breakfast ideas and can be mixed, matched, or prepped ahead to save time. One of the simplest options is overnight oats. Just combine rolled oats, milk or yogurt, a bit of honey, and your favorite fruits or seeds in a jar the night before, and by morning you've got a grab-and-go meal that's creamy, satisfying, and endlessly customizable.

Eggs are another breakfast superstar. Scrambled, boiled, poached, or made into muffins ahead of time, they cook quickly and keep you full longer thanks to their high protein content. Pair them with whole grain toast, avocado, or sautéed greens for a well-rounded meal that comes together in minutes. Smoothies are another fast favorite — simply blend up fruits, leafy greens, nut butter, and milk or water, and you've got a nutrient-packed drink that energizes and hydrates you for the day ahead.

If you prefer something heartier but still speedy, whole grain wraps or English muffins can be filled with eggs, spinach, cheese, or lean meats for a savory breakfast sandwich. You can make these in batches, freeze them, and reheat them in a flash. Or opt for a yogurt parfait layered with granola, berries, and a drizzle of maple syrup — a breakfast that feels indulgent but takes less than five minutes to prepare.

For those mornings when there's truly no time to cook, don't underestimate the power of thoughtful prep. Chopping fruit the night before, portioning out smoothie bags for the freezer, or hard-boiling eggs in advance makes it easier to stay on track even during the busiest weeks. Keeping healthy grab-and-go items on hand — like homemade energy bars, fruit, or nut butter packets — ensures that you always have something nourishing within reach.

It's also important to think about what "healthy" means for you. Some people need a hearty meal to jumpstart their metabolism, while others prefer something lighter and hydrating. The beauty of quick breakfasts is that they're flexible — you can tailor them to your preferences, dietary needs, and schedule without sacrificing quality or flavor.

Ultimately, breakfast is more than just fuel — it's the first decision you make each day about how you'll treat your body and yourself. Choosing something that's both quick and healthy doesn't have to be complicated. With the right habits, a few go-to ingredients, and a little creativity, breakfast becomes a ritual you look forward to — one that powers your morning and sets a positive tone for everything that follows.

Brunch Classics Reinvented

Brunch is where comfort meets creativity, where late mornings invite slow sips of coffee, and every dish feels like a small celebration. It's the perfect in-between meal — indulgent enough to satisfy, yet casual enough to invite experimentation. In this section, we take beloved brunch classics and give them a modern twist, breathing new life into familiar favorites without losing their comforting roots.

Take the humble pancake, for example. While the classic buttermilk version will always have a place on the table, reinventing it with whole grain flours, mashed bananas, or Greek yogurt can offer new textures and nutritional boosts. Add-ins like chia seeds, lemon zest, or a dash of cardamom elevate the flavor profile, and toppings can go from syrup to creative combos like almond butter and roasted berries or coconut cream and toasted nuts.

Avocado toast — a current brunch darling — also has endless potential. Instead of plain mashed avocado on bread, try layering it with roasted cherry tomatoes, poached eggs, feta crumbles, or spicy sriracha drizzle. Swap the bread for sweet potato slices, multi-seed crispbread, or even grilled polenta for a gluten-free or low-carb spin that still packs in the flavor and flair.

Eggs Benedict is another brunch icon that gets a fresh update with small changes. Think smoked salmon instead of ham, or roasted mushrooms for a vegetarian twist. Swap the traditional English muffin for a savory waffle or a slice of sourdough, and replace the hollandaise with a lighter yogurt-based sauce or avocado-lime crema. Reinvention doesn't mean losing the essence — it's about enhancing it with new textures, colors, and flavors.

Even the beloved omelet can evolve. Fold it around roasted veggies and fresh herbs, or go fusion-style with an Indian-spiced chickpea filling or a Korean kimchi-and-cheese blend. Serve it open-faced as a frittata or roll it into a wrap with greens and sauce for a brunch bite on the go. It's not about overcomplicating things — it's about exploring what else is possible within the familiar frame.

Let's not forget the sweeter side of brunch. French toast becomes extra special when made with brioche or sourdough and soaked in coconut milk or almond extract-spiked custard. Add a dollop of ricotta, a swirl of fruit compote, or a crunchy nut topping, and suddenly you've turned breakfast into a bakery-level treat. Muffins and scones, too, can be reimagined — incorporating unexpected ingredients like lavender, citrus peel, or shredded zucchini for freshness and character.

Reinventing brunch isn't about replacing what we love — it's about inviting curiosity into the kitchen. It's the joy of asking, "What if?" What if waffles were savory instead of sweet? What if we paired eggs with global flavors? What if we took grandma's coffee cake and gave it a cardamom kick?

Brunch is the perfect canvas for that kind of creativity. It's relaxed, social, and forgiving — a time to slow down, sip something warm, and savor the moment. So whether you're hosting a weekend gathering or treating yourself to something special, these reimagined brunch classics promise comfort with a twist — and a reminder that even the most traditional dishes can evolve into something beautifully new.

Smoothies, Bowls & Energy Boosters

Not all breakfasts are meant to be eaten with a fork and knife. Sometimes, the best way to start the day is with a spoonful of vibrant flavor or a sip of something cool, refreshing, and packed with energy. Smoothies, breakfast bowls, and other natural energy boosters are the modern answer to fueling your body fast — without compromising on nutrition or taste. They're perfect for busy mornings, post-workout replenishment, or even as a midday pick-me-up. In this section, we explore how you can blend, build, and boost your way to better mornings.

Smoothies are perhaps the quickest way to pack a powerful punch of vitamins, fiber, and protein into your morning routine. All you need is a good blender, a handful of ingredients, and a little creativity. A simple base of frozen banana or berries, a liquid like almond milk or coconut water, and a handful of leafy greens like spinach or kale can create a nutrient-rich powerhouse in minutes. Add-ins like chia seeds, flaxseeds, oats, protein powder, nut butter, or Greek yogurt can further enhance satiety and flavor while providing essential macronutrients to keep you going until your next meal.

But smoothies don't have to stay in a glass. Smoothie bowls have taken the spotlight for those who crave a bit more texture and visual satisfaction. By using less liquid and blending a thicker base, you can pour your smoothie into a bowl and layer it with colorful toppings — think sliced fruit, granola, shredded coconut, cacao nibs, or edible flowers. It becomes more than just breakfast; it becomes an experience, both nourishing and aesthetically delightful. Whether you're making an acai bowl bursting with antioxidants or a tropical mango-pineapple blend topped with hemp seeds and mint, the combinations are endless.

If you're someone who prefers something a little more hearty, breakfast energy bowls are the answer. These can be sweet or savory, warm or cold, and are designed to deliver slow-release energy throughout the day. You might start with a base of quinoa or oats, top it with roasted nuts, seeds, fruit, or a swirl of almond butter. Or go the savory route with a soft-boiled egg, steamed greens, and a sprinkle of pumpkin seeds over warm brown rice. These bowls are all about balance — combining protein, fiber, healthy fats, and complex carbs to create a complete meal in one dish.

Natural energy boosters go beyond the bowl, too. Think homemade energy bites made with dates, oats, peanut butter, and dark chocolate — easy to prep, store, and grab when you need a boost. Or try a morning tonic with warm lemon water, ginger, and turmeric for a metabolism kickstart. Even something as simple as a handful of raw almonds and a piece of fruit can offer a quick, clean burst of energy when you're short on time.

The beauty of these options lies in their flexibility. You can prep ingredients in advance, mix and match based on what you have, and customize flavors to your mood and nutritional needs. They're perfect for those who don't love heavy breakfasts or need something portable, and they offer a break from the traditional eggs-and-toast routine without sacrificing satisfaction.

So whether you're sipping a protein-packed smoothie, spooning into a vibrant bowl, or reaching for an energy bite on the run, these options prove that fast can still be fresh, and simple can still be powerful. Your mornings just got a whole lot more delicious — and a whole lot more energized.

Make-Ahead Morning Meals

Mornings don't always offer the luxury of time. Whether it's the rush to get kids out the door, an early work call, or simply the desire to hit snooze one more time, breakfast often becomes a hurried afterthought — or worse, skipped altogether. That's where make-ahead morning meals come to the rescue. With a little planning and preparation, you can have wholesome, satisfying breakfasts ready to grab and go, making your mornings smoother, healthier, and more enjoyable.

The beauty of make-ahead breakfasts is their ability to combine convenience with nourishment. You don't have to rely on boxed cereal or pre-packaged snacks when you've got meals already waiting in your fridge. From overnight oats and baked casseroles to breakfast burritos and muffins, these options are designed to save time while still fueling your day with balanced nutrition.

Overnight oats are perhaps the most popular make-ahead meal for a reason. They require no cooking, minimal ingredients, and endless possibilities for customization. Simply combine rolled oats with your favorite milk, a natural sweetener like honey or maple syrup, and toppings such as fruit, seeds, or nut butter. Let it sit overnight in the fridge, and by morning, you have a creamy, flavor-packed breakfast that's ready to eat cold or warmed up.

Egg-based dishes also lend themselves well to advance prep. Mini egg muffins made with whisked eggs, chopped veggies, cheese, and herbs can be baked in a muffin tin, stored in the fridge, and reheated quickly in the morning. They're protein-packed, portable, and perfect for busy weekdays. Or go a step further with breakfast burritos — filled with scrambled eggs, beans, veggies, and cheese, then wrapped in a tortilla and frozen. Just microwave and go.

For those who love a sweet start, baked oatmeal is a hearty and satisfying option. Mix oats with milk, mashed banana or applesauce, a touch of spice, and some fruit or nuts, then bake it into squares or portions that can be stored for the week. It's like having dessert for breakfast — only healthier and far more filling. You can also prep smoothie packs by portioning fruits and greens into freezer bags, ready to blend with liquid and add-ins each morning.

Even traditional breakfast favorites like pancakes and waffles can become make-ahead heroes. Make a batch over the weekend, then freeze them in single layers. Pop them in the toaster or oven during the week, and you'll have a hot, comforting breakfast in minutes. Add a dollop of yogurt, a sprinkle of seeds, or a drizzle of nut butter for a nutritious upgrade.

When prepping ahead, storage matters. Use airtight containers, label with dates, and keep a variety on hand to avoid breakfast boredom. Choose ingredients that hold well over time — oats, eggs, yogurt, cooked grains, roasted vegetables, and hardy fruits like apples and berries are all great choices. Make-ahead meals also support mindful eating; when breakfast is ready and waiting, you're less likely to reach for something processed or sugary in a pinch.

At the heart of it, make-ahead morning meals are about reclaiming your mornings. They turn frantic into calm, rushed into relaxed. With just a little prep, you can enjoy the comfort of a homemade meal without sacrificing time or energy. It's a small act of care that pays off in big ways — setting the tone for a day that begins not with stress, but with intention and nourishment.

Chapter 3
Bites & Nibbles – Snacks & Starters That Satisfy

Sometimes it's the little bites that bring the biggest joy. Whether you're entertaining guests, curbing mid-day hunger, or looking for a flavorful prelude to a meal, snacks and starters hold a special place in every kitchen. In this chapter, we celebrate the art of small plates — those delightful bites that are easy to prepare, fun to eat, and endlessly customizable.

From crispy finger foods to dips bursting with flavor, you'll find recipes here that are both satisfying and simple. Think golden fritters, savory pastries, vibrant spreads, spiced nuts, and skewered delights. These snacks aren't just quick fixes — they're carefully crafted to excite the taste buds and leave you wanting just one more bite.

You'll also explore globally inspired starters like Mediterranean hummus platters, Asian-style dumplings, and Latin American street snacks. Whether you're looking for something light and fresh or indulgent and cheesy, there's something for every craving and every occasion.

Snacks and starters are also perfect for experimenting with flavor combinations, textures, and presentation. Serve them at parties, picnics, or just for yourself on a cozy afternoon. With the right ingredients and a creative touch, even the smallest dish can make a lasting impression.

Dips & Spreads with a Kick

Dips and spreads may be small in portion, but they pack a powerful punch. They're the unsung heroes of the snack table, the secret stars of any appetizer platter, and often the first thing guests gravitate toward at a gathering. But we're not talking about bland, store-bought options here — we're diving into dips and spreads with a kick. These are bold, vibrant, flavor-loaded creations that awaken the palate and elevate even the simplest bite of bread, cracker, or veggie stick.

What makes a dip or spread truly memorable is balance — richness balanced with spice, creaminess lifted by acid, and heat mellowed by something cool. Ingredients like roasted garlic, chili flakes, harissa, jalapeños, smoked paprika, and sriracha bring layers of heat and depth, while herbs, citrus, and yogurt can brighten things up and keep flavors in check.

Let's start with hummus — the classic Middle Eastern spread made from chickpeas, tahini, lemon, and garlic. A traditional version is delicious on its own, but with a little creativity, it becomes something extraordinary. Add roasted red peppers and chili oil for a smoky twist, or blend in chipotle peppers for a rich, spicy upgrade. Want something unexpected? Try beetroot and horseradish hummus for an earthy flavor with a subtle bite and a stunning color that demands attention.

Guacamole is another crowd-pleaser that thrives on customization. Mash ripe avocados with lime juice, red onion, and salt, then turn up the heat with finely chopped serrano peppers, cayenne, or a dash of hot sauce. Toss in mango or pineapple for a tropical spin that plays sweet against spicy — perfect for tacos, toast, or straight from the spoon.

Yogurt-based spreads are cooling but don't have to be boring. Mix Greek yogurt with lemon zest, garlic, and chopped herbs for a fresh herbed dip, or stir in harissa paste for a spicy North African flair. Labneh — a strained yogurt cheese — makes a luxurious base for topping with olive oil, crushed chili flakes, and za'atar. Serve it with warm pita and watch it disappear fast.

If you love cheese, spicy cheese dips and spreads are a must. Pimento cheese, with sharp cheddar, mayonnaise, and diced pimentos, can be given a bold twist with jalapeños, smoked paprika, or hot sauce. For a warm option, melt cream cheese and pepper jack with green chiles and serve it bubbling as a spicy queso-style dip — ideal for tortilla chips or poured over nachos.

Don't forget bean dips and lentil spreads. Black beans blended with cumin, lime, garlic, and chipotle make a rich and smoky spread that pairs beautifully with corn chips or veggie sticks. A red lentil dip spiced with curry powder or chili oil offers a satisfying, protein-rich option with a Middle Eastern or Indian flair.

These dips and spreads don't just shine on the snack table — they're versatile enough to use as sandwich fillers, burger toppers, or even pasta sauces with a bit of thinning. They can turn a basic wrap into a flavor-packed meal or become the surprise element in a charcuterie board.

In the end, dips and spreads with a kick aren't just about heat — they're about boldness. They're about layering flavors, playing with textures, and creating something that surprises and satisfies with every bite. So grab a blender, a bowl, and a brave spirit — it's time to dip into something daring and delicious.

Finger Foods for Every Occasion

There's something irresistibly joyful about finger foods. They invite sharing, encourage mingling, and allow guests to graze freely without formality. Whether you're hosting a birthday party, a game night, a baby shower, or a cozy movie evening at home, finger foods fit effortlessly into every occasion. They're the bites that keep people coming back for more — no forks required, just flavor-packed morsels served with heart and ease.

Finger foods are the ultimate entertainers. They can be elegant or casual, hot or cold, savory or sweet. And while presentation matters, the key to great finger foods lies in their ability to deliver big taste in small packages. Think crispy, cheesy, spicy, or refreshing — miniature versions of crowd-pleasing favorites that can be popped into the mouth in one or two bites. What makes them extra special is their adaptability — many can be made ahead of time, prepped in large batches, or customized to suit dietary needs and preferences.

Take sliders, for instance. These mini sandwiches can be anything from classic cheeseburgers to pulled chicken with slaw, veggie patties with spicy mayo, or BBQ jackfruit for a plant-based option. Served on soft rolls or brioche buns, they're hearty, satisfying, and easy to dress up with sauces, pickles, or melted cheese. Arrange them on a platter, and they're instantly party-ready.

Skewers are another universal favorite. Whether it's grilled chicken satay, caprese skewers with mozzarella and cherry tomatoes, or fruit kabobs for a refreshing twist, food on a stick always draws attention. They're neat, easy to serve, and open to endless flavor profiles. Think global: pair marinated beef with chimichurri, shrimp with sweet chili sauce, or tofu cubes with peanut dipping sauce.

For something crispy and comforting, finger foods like spring rolls, samosas, or mini empanadas hit the spot. You can bake or fry them, fill them with veggies, meat, or cheese, and pair them with vibrant dips for extra flair. These kinds of bites often hold cultural significance too, bringing a taste of heritage to the table in an approachable, fun format.

Cheese and charcuterie boards are a modern finger food classic — not only beautiful but interactive. Let guests build their own bites with combinations of cheeses, cured meats, nuts, olives, fruits, and crackers. You can even personalize the board based on the occasion, season, or theme. Add some spicy mustard, fig jam, or roasted peppers for bold flavor accents.

Vegetable-based finger foods deserve just as much spotlight. Stuffed mushrooms, cucumber cups filled with herbed cream cheese, or sweet potato bites topped with avocado and salsa are just a few examples of healthy yet delicious options. They're light, bright, and offer a break from heavier bites — perfect for brunches, spa days, or more wellness-focused gatherings.

And let's not forget about sweet finger foods. Mini cupcakes, brownie bites, chocolate-covered strawberries, or cookie sandwiches are all finger-friendly and satisfy every sweet tooth without overindulging. You can even offer dessert platters where guests can mix and match their perfect little treat.

Ultimately, finger foods are more than just snacks — they're conversation starters, mood-lifters, and memory-makers. They let you bring variety to your spread without overwhelming yourself or your guests. Whether you're planning something spontaneous or pulling out all the stops for a big event, these small bites deliver in a big way.

So go ahead — roll, skewer, stuff, or stack. Finger foods are proof that sometimes, the best things really do come in small packages.

Light Bites with Big Flavor

Not every dish has to be heavy to leave a lasting impression. Sometimes, it's the light bites — the ones that surprise you with their boldness, their clever pairing of ingredients, or their vibrant freshness — that make the biggest impact. "Light Bites with Big Flavor" is all about crafting snacks and small plates that are easy on the stomach but rich in taste, texture, and creativity.

These aren't your average appetizers. They're the kinds of dishes that wake up the palate, refresh your senses, and keep you coming back for just one more nibble. Designed for casual grazing, elegant entertaining, or even mid-day snacking, light bites can be nourishing and satisfying without ever feeling heavy or overindulgent.

What gives these dishes their punch is smart flavor layering. A slice of toasted baguette becomes a flavor bomb when topped with whipped feta, roasted cherry tomatoes, and a drizzle of balsamic glaze. A single rice paper roll filled with crisp vegetables, fresh herbs, and a touch of mango becomes unforgettable when paired with a bold peanut-lime dipping sauce. Or consider a delicate cucumber round — so simple, yet so impactful when topped with lemon-zest yogurt, smoked salmon, and capers.

Acidity, herbs, spice, and umami are your best friends when it comes to building big flavor in small portions. A squeeze of lemon or lime can brighten up any dish. Fresh herbs like basil, cilantro, dill, or mint add freshness and aroma. A pinch of chili flakes or a dab of sriracha can take a mellow bite to the next level. Even a sprinkle of flaky sea salt or toasted seeds can turn a humble bite into a gourmet moment.

Global influences shine in this category too. Mediterranean-inspired bites like marinated olives, roasted red pepper tapenade on crostini, or chickpea salad cups bring sunny, layered flavors with minimal effort. Asian-inspired lettuce wraps, stuffed with seasoned tofu, shrimp, or chicken, offer a refreshing crunch and a spicy-sweet finish when paired with the right dipping sauce. Middle Eastern-style falafel balls served with a tahini drizzle, or small dolmas with lemon yogurt, offer a satisfying savory edge while remaining light and portable.

Light bites also open up space for creativity. You can play with presentation — serve ingredients in little jars, skewered on picks, tucked into endive leaves, or neatly lined on slate boards. The experience becomes not just about eating, but about enjoying the colors, shapes, and textures of food.

Another advantage of light bites is their versatility. They work as appetizers, tapas, snacks, or even part of a casual dinner where a variety of small plates come together to form a complete meal. They're easy to batch-prepare, often served cold or at room temperature, and can be both elegant and approachable at the same time.

These bites are especially perfect for those looking to eat more mindfully — they let you taste and savor without overdoing it. And because they rely on quality ingredients and thoughtful seasoning, they never feel like a compromise. Instead, they feel intentional, flavorful, and full of personality.

So whether you're curating a light lunch spread, assembling a snack board for friends, or just looking for that perfect mid-afternoon bite, remember: light doesn't have to mean boring. With the right ingredients and a little imagination, you can pack a world of flavor into the tiniest, most delightful morsels.

Savory Pastries & Mini Sandwiches

There's something universally satisfying about holding a warm, flaky pastry or a perfectly portioned mini sandwich in your hand — a little bundle of comfort, flavor, and joy. Savory pastries and mini sandwiches are timeless finger foods that offer endless variety, elegance, and convenience. Whether you're hosting a brunch, planning a picnic, or simply craving something cozy, these bite-sized delights can be as refined or as rustic as you want them to be — and they always deliver.

Savory pastries are the perfect union of crisp, golden crust and rich, flavorful filling. Puff pastry, with its buttery layers, serves as a magical base that can be filled, folded, twisted, or rolled to suit nearly any occasion. From classic spinach and feta triangles to spicy sausage rolls, from mushroom and cheese pinwheels to caramelized onion tarts, there's no shortage of delicious combinations. Even store-bought pastry dough can be transformed into something spectacular with the right filling — think sun-dried tomatoes and goat cheese, or pesto with roasted vegetables.

What makes these pastries so appealing is their versatility. You can serve them hot or at room temperature, and they're easy to prepare in batches ahead of time. Some recipes even freeze beautifully, letting you bake fresh as needed. And they're not just for breakfast or brunch — pair them with a simple salad or soup, and you've got a complete meal in hand-held form.

Then there are mini sandwiches — charming, satisfying, and endlessly adaptable. These aren't the tired, soggy triangles from childhood lunchboxes; they're fresh, vibrant, and packed with flavor.

Imagine bite-sized croissants filled with chicken salad and arugula, or petite brioche buns stuffed with roast beef, horseradish cream, and crispy shallots. Even simple fillings like cucumber with herbed cream cheese, egg salad with a twist of paprika, or smoked salmon with dill butter can feel elevated when tucked neatly between soft, pillowy bread.

Mini sandwiches are perfect for parties because they're easy to assemble, hold well on a platter, and please a crowd with minimal fuss. You can vary the breads — from sliders and baguette slices to wraps and savory muffins — and cater to different diets with vegetarian, vegan, or gluten-free options. Serve a mix of warm and cold varieties to keep things interesting and balanced.

Presentation plays a big role here, too. Stack them high, layer them with parchment, or thread mini sandwiches onto skewers for a modern take. Add a garnish like fresh herbs, pickled onions, or tiny skewers to hold them together, and suddenly you've got gourmet-level appetizers that are as pleasing to the eyes as they are to the palate.

What's most special about savory pastries and mini sandwiches is their ability to feel both nostalgic and fresh. They bring back memories of family gatherings, afternoon teas, and holiday buffets, while still offering room for creativity and reinvention. With a few simple ingredients and a touch of imagination, these small bites can become the star of your table.

So whether you're hosting a formal event or just preparing a weekend treat, these pastries and sandwiches offer the perfect balance of comfort, convenience, and crave-worthy flavor — proving that when it comes to good food, small really can be mighty.

Chapter 4
Comfort in a Bowl – Soups & Stews

There's something undeniably soothing about a warm bowl held in your hands — steam rising, aromas swirling, and flavors that seem to wrap around your soul. This chapter is dedicated to that kind of comfort. Soups and stews are more than just meals; they're memories simmered slowly, often passed down through generations, bringing warmth to both body and spirit.

From hearty stews that stick to your ribs to delicate broths that heal from within, you'll find recipes here for every mood and season. We'll guide you through crafting deep, flavorful bases, layering spices and aromatics, and using everyday ingredients to create extraordinary results. Whether you're craving a rustic lentil stew, a classic chicken noodle, a velvety tomato soup, or something globally inspired like Thai coconut curry soup — this chapter has it all.

Soups and stews are also perfect for meal prepping, feeding a crowd, or simply curling up on the couch after a long day. They're forgiving, flexible, and open to creative improvisation — add your favorite vegetables, swap proteins, or toss in yesterday's leftovers. A good soup doesn't judge.

Pair them with crusty bread, a drizzle of cream, or fresh herbs on top, and you've got a dish that feels like home. So grab your pot and your ladle — comfort awaits, one simmering bowl at a time.

Hearty Stews for Chilly Nights

There's something deeply comforting about a pot of stew bubbling away on a chilly night. It's the kind of meal that wraps itself around you like a blanket — warm, hearty, and full of depth. Whether it's a slow-simmered beef stew, a fragrant lentil medley, or a rustic chicken and vegetable concoction, stews have a way of turning simple ingredients into something soul-satisfying. These dishes are more than just food — they're tradition, nourishment, and warmth all in one bowl.

The magic of stew lies in its simplicity. You don't need fancy ingredients or complicated techniques. All you need is a pot, a little patience, and the willingness to let flavors slowly meld together into something extraordinary. Stews are forgiving, flexible, and endlessly adaptable to what's in your pantry or fridge. Leftover vegetables, a handful of herbs, some beans or lentils, and a protein of your choice can come together to create something that tastes like it took all day — even if it didn't.

A good stew is built in layers. Start with aromatics — onions, garlic, leeks, or celery — sautéed gently until fragrant. This foundation sets the stage for deeper flavors to develop. Then come the hearty elements: chunks of meat that brown beautifully before being simmered to tenderness, or legumes that absorb the surrounding flavors as they soften. Root vegetables like potatoes, carrots, parsnips, or turnips add substance and sweetness, while herbs like thyme, rosemary, or bay leaves provide the earthy notes that stews are known for.

Liquids bring it all together. Whether it's a rich beef stock, a light vegetable broth, a splash of wine, or even coconut milk for a creamy finish, the liquid should complement your chosen ingredients and simmer low and slow until everything is tender and cohesive. That's when the real magic happens — when the flavors deepen, the textures soften, and the kitchen fills with the kind of aroma that tells you something special is on the stove.

Stews also invite cultural exploration. A Moroccan tagine with chickpeas and preserved lemons, a Hungarian goulash with paprika and tender beef, or a Caribbean-inspired stew with sweet potatoes and allspice — each variation tells a story and brings new tastes to your table. Don't be afraid to experiment with global flavors or your own spice blends. Stews are a canvas for creativity.

And let's not forget about the accompaniments. A slice of crusty bread, a bowl of rice, or a fluffy pile of mashed potatoes can elevate a stew from satisfying to sublime. The contrast of textures — soft, savory stew against a firm, chewy starch — is what makes every bite dynamic and fulfilling.

The beauty of stews is that they're made to share. They bring people together, simmering quietly in the background while life happens. You can make them in large batches, freeze portions for busy nights, or let the leftovers deepen in flavor overnight. In many ways, stew is the definition of comfort food — slow, hearty, honest, and deeply nourishing.

So when the weather turns cold and the days grow short, lean into the timeless ritual of making stew. It's not just about staying warm — it's about feeding the body and the spirit, one tender spoonful at a time.

Clear Soups & Broths for Light Days

Some days call for simplicity — for something light, warming, and gentle on the body. On those days, nothing satisfies quite like a clear soup or a delicate broth. Whether you're recovering from indulgence, seeking a nourishing reset, or simply craving something clean and comforting, clear soups offer flavor without the heaviness. They're the quiet achievers of the culinary world: subtle yet deeply satisfying, restorative yet incredibly versatile.

Unlike their thicker, stew-like counterparts, clear soups focus on clarity — both in appearance and taste. A well-made broth is like a blank canvas, delicately infused with aromatics and ingredients that enhance without overwhelming. The result is a soup that feels clean and wholesome, yet still rich in flavor. It's comfort food in its purest, most elegant form.

The foundation of any great clear soup is the broth. Homemade broths — whether chicken, beef, vegetable, or even fish — are ideal because they allow full control over salt, fat, and depth of flavor. They're surprisingly simple to make: just simmer bones or vegetables with water, a few herbs, garlic, onion, and perhaps a splash of vinegar for a few hours. Skim off any foam, strain carefully, and you're left with liquid gold. For convenience, store-bought broths work too — just opt for low-sodium versions so you can season to your taste.

Once you have a flavorful base, the possibilities are endless. Add thinly sliced vegetables like carrots, zucchini, mushrooms, or cabbage for texture and color. A handful of spinach or kale right before serving adds a gentle nutritional boost. Toss in some noodles, rice, or quinoa for a light meal that still satisfies. Or keep it minimalist with nothing more than broth, herbs, and a sprinkle of scallions or toasted sesame seeds.

Clear soups also lend themselves beautifully to global flavors. Try a classic miso soup with tofu and wakame, or a Vietnamese-inspired pho made with aromatic spices like star anise, cloves, and cinnamon. A simple egg drop soup — with silky ribbons of egg floating in seasoned broth — can be whipped up in minutes and tastes like home in a bowl. And a lemony Greek avgolemono, made with broth, egg, lemon juice, and rice, is the perfect example of how simple ingredients can deliver bold, comforting flavors.

These soups are ideal when you want something soothing without feeling weighed down. They're wonderful for busy days when you need quick nourishment, or for quiet evenings when you're winding down. They're easy to digest, hydrating, and packed with potential for immune-boosting ingredients like garlic, ginger, turmeric, and herbs.

Presentation also plays a lovely role. A bowl of clear soup garnished with fresh cilantro, a few chili flakes, a swirl of sesame oil, or a wedge of lime looks just as beautiful as it tastes. It invites you to slow down, to sip, to savor — a mindful break in a busy day.

Clear soups and broths may be light, but they never lack in impact. They prove that a handful of thoughtful ingredients, combined with care and patience, can create something deeply nourishing and unexpectedly elegant. So next time you're seeking comfort in its most delicate form, reach for a clear soup — and let its simplicity restore both body and mind.

Global Soup Delights

There's something universally comforting about soup — a dish that transcends borders, cultures, and languages. No matter where you are in the world, there's likely a beloved local soup simmering with history, flavor, and tradition. In this section, we celebrate Global Soup Delights, a flavorful journey through broths and bowls that speak of faraway lands and cherished family recipes. From spicy to soothing, rich to refreshing, these international soups bring the world to your kitchen — one spoonful at a time.

Let's begin in Southeast Asia, where pho, Vietnam's iconic noodle soup, warms hearts and bellies alike. Made with a deeply aromatic broth simmered for hours with beef bones, star anise, cinnamon, cloves, and ginger, pho is served with thin rice noodles, tender meat, and a fresh scattering of herbs, bean sprouts, lime, and chili. It's more than a dish — it's an experience of balance, patience, and vibrant customization.

Traveling west, we find the bold and colorful flavors of Mexico in pozole. This traditional hominy-based soup is often made with pork or chicken and seasoned with garlic, chili peppers, and oregano. It's served with a medley of garnishes — sliced radish, shredded lettuce, lime wedges, and crunchy tortilla strips — turning each bowl into a mini feast.

In West Africa, peanut soup is a hearty, soul-satisfying staple. Combining ground peanuts (or peanut butter) with tomatoes, onions, garlic, ginger, and often chicken, this dish is rich, creamy, and spicy all at once. Served over rice or eaten as-is, it's a celebration of depth and comfort in every bite.

Then there's the beloved ramen from Japan — a noodle soup that comes in countless variations. Whether it's a shoyu (soy sauce) broth, miso-based, or a deeply savory tonkotsu (pork bone) broth, ramen brings together chewy noodles, savory meats, soft-boiled eggs, and an array of toppings like scallions, seaweed, and sesame seeds. It's the perfect harmony of texture and umami — and a bowl that invites slow, satisfying slurps.

Closer to the Mediterranean, we have the Greek avgolemono — a lemony chicken and rice soup thickened with eggs. Tangy, creamy, and comforting, it's often served during colder months or to soothe the soul during times of illness or celebration. It shows how a handful of ingredients can create something truly elegant and deeply satisfying.

India offers a range of soup-like dishes, but one of the most beloved is rasam, a thin, spicy, tamarind-based soup enriched with tomatoes, garlic, mustard seeds, and curry leaves. Often served as a starter or over rice, rasam is known for its warming, digestive properties and its bright, tangy flavor.

Let's not forget Eastern Europe's borscht — a beetroot-based soup often served with sour cream and fresh dill. Though traditionally made with beef or pork, vegetarian versions are equally popular. Its vibrant color and sweet-earthy flavor make it stand out, especially during colder seasons when its warmth is most welcome.

What unites all these global soups is their ability to tell a story. They reflect the ingredients of the land, the customs of the people, and the memories of countless kitchens. They're often humble in origin — born from necessity, shaped by tradition — yet capable of delivering gourmet-level satisfaction.

Exploring global soup delights is a delicious way to connect with other cultures and expand your palate. So go ahead — open your spice drawer, try something new, and let your kitchen become a melting pot of global flavor and love.

Sides & Breads That Pair Perfectly

No great bowl of soup is truly complete without the perfect sidekick. Whether it's a crusty wedge of bread begging to be dipped or a flavorful side that enhances the main dish, the right pairing turns a simple bowl of soup into a well-rounded meal. In this section, we celebrate Sides & Breads That Pair Perfectly — the companions that add texture, contrast, and comfort to every steaming spoonful.

Let's start with bread — the classic partner-in-crime to soup. There's nothing quite like tearing off a piece of warm, crusty bread and dipping it into a savory broth. A good loaf of artisan sourdough or a crusty baguette absorbs flavor beautifully, softening just enough without disintegrating. For cream-based soups, like chowders or bisques, a dense, chewy bread like ciabatta or a country loaf offers a hearty contrast to the silky textures of the soup.

Flatbreads are another excellent pairing, especially when you're exploring global flavors. Think of pillowy naan alongside an Indian lentil soup, or garlic pita wedges with a Mediterranean tomato-lentil broth. Even store-bought options can be elevated with a quick toast in the oven, a brush of olive oil, or a sprinkle of herbs and sea salt. For a fun twist, try making homemade focaccia or cheesy breadsticks — great for tearing, dipping, or simply snacking between bites.

Cornbread, with its subtle sweetness and crumbly texture, pairs wonderfully with spicy or smoky soups like chili or black bean stew. Whether baked in a skillet or muffin tin, it brings a satisfying contrast to bold flavors and adds a touch of Southern charm to the table. Add jalapeños, cheddar, or herbs to the mix for an extra kick.

Beyond bread, hearty sides can complete the meal and turn a simple soup into a more filling, dynamic experience. A lightly dressed salad with peppery arugula, citrus segments, and a zesty vinaigrette pairs beautifully with a rich creamy soup — the freshness cuts through the richness and refreshes the palate. Roasted vegetables, like honey-glazed carrots or garlic-parmesan cauliflower, bring both warmth and substance, making them great companions to lighter, broth-based soups.

Grains and starches also make for smart sides. A scoop of wild rice or a small serving of herbed couscous can be served on the side or stirred directly into the soup bowl. Quinoa salads, farro with roasted vegetables, or even simple buttered noodles give you the flexibility to adjust portions while adding variety and nutrition.

For a more elevated touch, consider stuffed mushrooms, savory hand pies, or small open-faced sandwiches (known as tartines). These offer richness and flavor in small packages and can be customized to complement the soup's profile — mushroom and thyme for an earthy stew, smoked salmon and dill for a light potato soup, or caramelized onion and goat cheese for a roasted tomato base.

What's important is balance — matching light with bold, creamy with crisp, and spicy with cool. Sides and breads give you a chance to create contrast, add a tactile element, and bring more texture and color to the plate.

In the end, these pairings are more than just accompaniments — they're extensions of the meal itself. They add warmth, nourishment, and variety, turning every bowl of soup into a true dining experience. So next time you ladle something comforting into a bowl, don't forget the finishing touch — that perfect side or slice that makes the moment complete.

Chapter 5
Fresh & Flavorful – Salads Beyond the Basics

Gone are the days when salads were just a side of limp greens and bottled dressing. In this chapter, we're tossing tradition aside and diving into vibrant, satisfying salads that steal the spotlight. These are dishes that burst with color, texture, and bold flavor — hearty enough to stand alone, yet elegant enough to accompany any main course.

Salads are the perfect canvas for creativity. Think juicy fruits paired with peppery greens, crisp vegetables mingling with grains, or charred proteins layered over creamy dressings and crunchy toppings. Here, you'll discover how to build a salad that's balanced in taste and nutrition, with just the right mix of freshness, crunch, acidity, and richness.

From Mediterranean chickpea bowls and Asian sesame slaws to warm roasted vegetable salads and zesty citrus mixes — every recipe in this chapter is designed to nourish and excite. We'll also walk you through homemade dressings, flavor-boosting add-ins, and tips for prepping ingredients ahead so you can assemble meals in minutes.

Whether you're packing a healthy lunch, impressing dinner guests, or simply craving something light and wholesome, these salads go far beyond the basics. They're proof that with the right ingredients, a salad can be much more than just leafy greens — it can be the star of your plate.

Green Goodness: Leafy Salads

Leafy salads are often underestimated — seen as a side note or an obligatory nod to health. But in truth, a well-made green salad can be a showstopper. It's the kind of dish that can be light and refreshing or bold and satisfying, depending on how you build it. In this section, Green Goodness: Leafy Salads, we celebrate the vibrant world of greens and the endless possibilities they offer when paired with thoughtful textures, flavors, and dressings.

The foundation of any great salad starts with the greens. From delicate butter lettuce to peppery arugula, earthy spinach to hearty kale, the variety available offers different textures, tastes, and nutritional profiles. Mixing greens adds complexity and visual appeal — try combining crisp romaine with radicchio for crunch and color, or baby spinach with watercress for a peppery punch.

What makes a leafy salad memorable, however, is everything that surrounds the greens. Layering textures and flavors is key. Think creamy avocado against crisp cucumber, juicy orange segments paired with toasted almonds, or tangy goat cheese crumbled over sweet cherry tomatoes. Don't be afraid to play with contrast — soft with crunchy, sweet with salty, bitter with bright. These pairings keep each bite interesting and satisfying.

Proteins like grilled chicken, boiled eggs, chickpeas, lentils, or tofu can easily turn a simple green salad into a hearty, balanced meal. Add grains like quinoa, farro, or bulgur to bulk it up even more without losing the refreshing essence of a salad. Roasted vegetables — from beets and carrots to zucchini or butternut squash — bring warmth and a satisfying earthiness that pairs beautifully with greens.

Then there's the unsung hero of the salad: the dressing. A dressing can elevate your greens from ordinary to irresistible. A classic vinaigrette with olive oil, vinegar, mustard, and herbs is always a good place to start. But you can go far beyond that — tahini dressings with lemon and garlic, creamy avocado-lime blends, honey-mustard vinaigrettes, or miso-ginger sauces can all bring your salad to life. The key is balance: fat for richness, acid for brightness, and seasoning to tie it all together.

Even small touches make a big difference — a sprinkle of seeds, a handful of croutons, shaved parmesan, or dried cranberries. These final flourishes not only enhance flavor and texture but also make the dish visually appealing, turning a pile of greens into something truly enticing.

Leafy salads also adapt effortlessly to the seasons. In spring, tender greens with strawberries and a light citrus dressing feel bright and energizing. In fall, swap in roasted squash, apples, and a maple-balsamic drizzle. Even winter offers opportunities with hearty greens like kale and cabbage, paired with orange segments, nuts, and warming spices. There's no season that doesn't welcome a beautiful bowl of greens.

The beauty of green salads is their simplicity and flexibility. You don't need a recipe — just a sense of balance and creativity. Use what you have, taste as you go, and build layers thoughtfully. The result is a dish that feels clean, nourishing, and utterly satisfying.

So the next time you think of salad as something secondary, think again. With the right mix of greens, textures, and flavor, a leafy salad becomes something to savor — a bowl full of green goodness that's anything but ordinary.

Grain Bowls & Hearty Bases

Grain bowls have become a beloved staple in modern kitchens, and for good reason. They're vibrant, filling, and endlessly adaptable — a perfect blend of taste, texture, and nutrition in one balanced bowl. With a sturdy, wholesome base like quinoa, brown rice, farro, or bulgur, you can build a meal that feels both grounding and energizing. Grain Bowls & Hearty Bases are where the art of salad meets the science of satisfaction, combining whole grains with proteins, veggies, and bold dressings to create dishes that truly fuel the body.

At the core of a grain bowl is, of course, the grain — and the choices are as varied as the flavors they support. Quinoa is light, fluffy, and rich in protein, making it a go-to for those seeking plant-based nutrition. Brown rice offers a nutty flavor and chewy texture, while farro adds a satisfying bite and depth. Couscous and bulgur, quicker to prepare, soak up dressings beautifully and provide a soft, comforting base. These grains are not just carriers — they bring their own unique taste and character to the table.

Once the grain is cooked, the real fun begins. Add layers of color, crunch, and contrast with fresh or roasted vegetables — cherry tomatoes, cucumbers, bell peppers, sweet potatoes, beets, or charred broccoli. Don't be afraid to mix raw and cooked elements for a dynamic bite. A spoonful of something pickled or fermented — like kimchi, sauerkraut, or quick-pickled onions — can add brightness and tang that balances richer elements.

Protein is another key component that turns a grain bowl into a full, satisfying meal. Grilled chicken, steak, shrimp, or roasted salmon work beautifully, but plant-based proteins like tofu, tempeh, chickpeas, black beans, or lentils can be just as hearty. A soft-boiled egg or a sprinkle of feta or halloumi adds creaminess and indulgence without overwhelming the dish.

The magic, though, often lies in the toppings and finishing touches. A drizzle of tahini dressing, a spoonful of hummus, a swirl of pesto, or a squeeze of lemon can bring everything together. Fresh herbs like cilantro, mint, or parsley offer freshness and fragrance. Toasted nuts or seeds — almonds, sunflower seeds, pepitas — bring the crunch that takes a bowl from good to unforgettable.

The best part about grain bowls is that they welcome customization. You can make them warm or cold, spicy or mild, Mediterranean-inspired or Asian-infused. They're perfect for meal prep too — cook a large batch of grains, roast a tray of veggies, and store your toppings separately so you can assemble a fresh bowl in minutes throughout the week.

And while grain bowls are inherently nutritious, they never feel like a sacrifice. They're filling, flavorful, and packed with diverse textures that make every bite interesting. They also encourage mindful eating — when everything is arranged in a bowl with intention and variety, you naturally slow down to savor it all.

Whether you're nourishing your body after a workout, preparing a no-fuss lunch, or serving a casual yet elegant dinner, grain bowls with hearty bases offer a delicious and dependable option. They remind us that real food doesn't have to be complicated — just honest, colorful, and made with care.

Protein-Packed Salad Meals

Gone are the days when salads were seen as light side dishes or rabbit food. Today's salads are robust, energizing, and satisfying — especially when packed with protein. Protein-Packed Salad Meals are built to fuel your day, keep you fuller for longer, and deliver the perfect balance of nutrients in a fresh and flavorful format. Whether you're a meat-lover, vegetarian, or somewhere in between, these salads prove that healthy eating doesn't mean giving up on taste or satisfaction.

The key to building a protein-rich salad is starting with intention. Instead of thinking of greens as the main event, treat protein as the star of the show and layer your ingredients around it. This approach not only makes your salads more filling, but it also adds texture, heartiness, and flavor depth. From grilled chicken and steak to lentils, beans, and tofu, the options are vast and flexible for every palate and dietary style.

For meat eaters, grilled or roasted chicken is a go-to for good reason — it's lean, versatile, and pairs well with almost any dressing or vegetable. Sliced steak adds richness and bold flavor, especially when paired with arugula, roasted peppers, and a balsamic glaze. Shredded turkey, salmon, or even boiled eggs are all excellent additions to boost protein and make your salad feel like a complete meal.

If you're exploring plant-based proteins, legumes are your best friend. Chickpeas, black beans, white beans, and lentils not only offer a hearty bite but also soak up flavor from dressings and herbs beautifully. For added texture and protein, consider grilled tofu, tempeh, or even edamame. These ingredients not only balance the meal nutritionally but also bring in delicious umami and satisfying chew.

Cheese can also contribute both flavor and protein — think crumbled feta, shaved parmesan, cubes of cheddar, or a handful of cottage cheese for creaminess. Nuts and seeds, like almonds, pumpkin seeds, or hemp hearts, bring a nutritional bonus of healthy fats and additional protein, plus that crave-worthy crunch that makes every bite exciting.

What pulls it all together, though, is a strong combination of vegetables, grains, and dressings. Roasted sweet potatoes, grilled zucchini, and marinated mushrooms make great companions to your protein source. A small serving of whole grains like farro, quinoa, or brown rice helps to round out the plate and adds a gentle, nutty base. Dressings should enhance — not overpower — your ingredients. Tangy vinaigrettes, creamy tahini blends, or zesty citrus-based dressings are all wonderful choices.

One of the best things about protein-packed salads is how well they lend themselves to meal prep. You can batch-cook proteins and grains at the beginning of the week, chop veggies in advance, and store your components separately. When it's time to eat, just assemble your bowl, toss on your favorite dressing, and enjoy a fresh, nourishing meal in minutes.

These salad meals work for every occasion — a quick lunch between meetings, a post-workout recovery bowl, or even a weeknight dinner that doesn't require turning on the oven. They're adaptable to seasonal produce and leftovers, making them both eco-friendly and budget-conscious.

At the heart of it, protein-packed salads are about balance — delivering everything your body needs in a dish that's light enough to feel fresh, yet hearty enough to satisfy. So don't be surprised if they become a staple in your weekly rotation. They're colorful, creative, and endlessly customizable — proof that salad can be the star of your plate.

Dressings, Toppings & Crunch

If the greens and grains are the base of a great salad, then the dressings, toppings, and crunch are the flair — the final touch that transforms it from good to unforgettable. These finishing elements are where creativity meets contrast, turning simple ingredients into something layered, textured, and bursting with flavor.

Let's start with dressings. A well-crafted dressing brings harmony to a salad or grain bowl, tying together ingredients and adding moisture, acidity, and richness. The best dressings strike a balance between fat, acid, sweetness, and salt. Olive oil and lemon juice with a pinch of sea salt? A classic. But the options are endless. Try balsamic vinegar with honey and mustard, tahini with garlic and lemon, or a creamy yogurt and dill blend. Asian-inspired dressings made with soy sauce, rice vinegar, sesame oil, and a touch of maple syrup deliver umami and brightness all in one drizzle.

Homemade dressings are easy to make in small batches and store in the fridge for days. Shaking them up in a jar or whisking them in a bowl takes just minutes, and you have full control over the ingredients — no mystery preservatives or hidden sugars here. Plus, experimenting with flavors is part of the fun. Want heat? Add chili flakes or sriracha. Looking for something tangy? A splash of apple cider vinegar or fresh citrus can wake up an entire dish.

Once your base is dressed, it's time for the toppings. These are the pops of color, bursts of flavor, and bites of interest that make every forkful exciting. Soft elements like crumbled cheeses, sliced avocado, sun-dried tomatoes, or roasted red peppers add richness and contrast. Pickled onions, olives, or capers contribute saltiness and brightness, enhancing the overall flavor profile.

And then there's the crunch. Never underestimate the power of texture in a dish. That satisfying bite of something crisp — it's what makes you go back for more. Toasted nuts and seeds are reliable favorites. Almond slivers, sunflower seeds, pumpkin seeds, walnuts, and pecans all offer nutty depth while packing a nutritional punch. You can candy them with maple syrup and a pinch of cayenne for a sweet-spicy twist or roast them with sea salt for a savory touch.

Croutons are the ultimate classic crunch — but even here, there's room to explore. Make your own with leftover bread tossed in olive oil, garlic, and herbs, or try pita chips, chickpea crisps, or roasted lentils for a different texture. Shredded raw vegetables like carrots, fennel, or cabbage also bring a natural crispness to the mix, making your bowl feel more substantial and dynamic.

The beauty of dressings, toppings, and crunch is that they allow you to personalize every meal. One bowl can become a dozen different dishes depending on the flavors you layer over the top. They give you a chance to play, to express your style, and to turn even the most basic ingredients into something crave-worthy.

So next time you build a salad or grain bowl, don't stop at the base. Add a drizzle, sprinkle, and crunch — and watch your dish come alive.

Chapter 6
Weeknight Wonders – Easy Main Courses

Busy evenings call for simple solutions — but that doesn't mean sacrificing flavor or satisfaction. In this chapter, we're all about creating easy, reliable, and downright delicious main courses that fit perfectly into your weeknight routine. Whether you're feeding a hungry family or cooking for one, these recipes are designed to make dinnertime stress-free and enjoyable.

From skillet meals and stir-fries to sheet pan dinners and quick pastas, every recipe focuses on minimal prep, everyday ingredients, and maximum flavor. These dishes are made to be weeknight-friendly — quick to prepare, easy to clean up, and hearty enough to keep everyone at the table happy.

You'll find options for meat lovers, vegetarians, and everyone in between. Think lemon garlic chicken with roasted veggies, creamy mushroom risotto, zesty taco bowls, or even a build-your-own stir-fry night. These meals are not only comforting and satisfying, but they also offer flexibility — allowing you to swap proteins, adjust spices, or use whatever you already have in the fridge.

This chapter will also offer smart cooking tips like batch prepping, using leftovers creatively, and building a weekly dinner plan. Because when your meals are quick, healthy, and full of flavor, your weeknights turn from rushed to rewarding.

So roll up your sleeves — it's time to turn "What's for dinner?" into your favorite question of the day.

One-Pot and One-Pan Recipes

There's something deeply satisfying about cooking a delicious, nourishing meal using just one pot or pan. It's the kind of approach that says, "I've got you covered," especially after a long day when the idea of scrubbing multiple dishes is the last thing on your mind. One-Pot and One-Pan Recipes are the everyday hero of the home kitchen — efficient, comforting, and brimming with flavor, without the mess.

What makes these recipes so beloved is their simplicity. You don't need fancy techniques or an arsenal of tools — just a single, trusty pot or pan and a little layering of ingredients. These meals are perfect for weeknights, meal prepping, or feeding a hungry family without spending hours at the stove. And despite their simplicity, they're anything but boring.

Let's start with one-pot meals. Think hearty soups, creamy pastas, simmering stews, and flavorful rice dishes — all cooked together so the ingredients meld into one cohesive, comforting whole. A good one-pot pasta, for example, lets you cook noodles right in the sauce along with vegetables and protein, so everything absorbs flavor and comes together at once. Not only does it save on time and cleanup, but it also creates a dish that tastes like it's been simmering for hours — even if it only took twenty minutes.

Risottos, chili, curry, and braised dishes all shine in a one-pot format. Sauté your aromatics first to build flavor, then layer in your ingredients gradually, letting each step build on the last. The result is a meal with depth and richness, all in a single vessel. And with fewer dishes to clean, you can spend more time actually enjoying your dinner — and maybe even a second helping.

One-pan recipes offer the same convenience, but with a focus on roasting, baking, or sautéing everything together on a sheet tray or large skillet. They're especially great for meals where you want different textures — crispy edges, tender centers, and a bit of caramelization. Sheet pan dinners can be as simple as seasoned chicken thighs with root vegetables, or as creative as marinated tofu with rainbow bell peppers and sesame glaze.

The key to success with one-pan meals is arranging your ingredients thoughtfully. Group those that cook at similar rates, and add faster-cooking items toward the end. A splash of olive oil, a handful of herbs, and a few lemon slices can transform even the most basic ingredient lineup into a vibrant, flavorful feast. And don't be afraid to play with global spices — a sprinkle of cumin, smoked paprika, curry powder, or za'atar can take your dish in a whole new direction.

What's wonderful about these meals is how customizable they are. Have leftover veggies? Toss them in. Need to use up cooked rice or beans? Mix them right into the pot. These recipes are forgiving and flexible — perfect for reducing waste, using pantry staples, and adapting to whatever ingredients you have on hand.

At their heart, one-pot and one-pan recipes are about more than convenience — they're about ease without sacrifice. They prove that with just one piece of cookware, you can create something warm, satisfying, and packed with flavor. So the next time you're short on time or energy but still want something homemade, let a single pot or pan do the work. You'll be surprised by how much you can create — and how little cleanup you'll have to face.

Quick Stove-Top Favorites

When you're short on time but still want something homemade, nothing beats the speed and satisfaction of a quick stove-top meal. Quick Stove-Top Favorites are the reliable weeknight warriors of the kitchen — fast, flexible, and full of flavor. Whether you're whipping up dinner in under 30 minutes or sneaking in a hot lunch between meetings, these dishes deliver comfort and nourishment without requiring hours of prep or a pile of dishes.

The secret to great stove-top cooking is knowing how to build flavor fast. A hot pan, a splash of oil, and some aromatic ingredients — like garlic, onion, or ginger — can transform a simple base into something crave-worthy. Once the aromatics hit the heat, your kitchen fills with that inviting smell that says, "Something good is happening." From there, it's just about layering quick-cooking proteins, veggies, grains, or sauces to complete the dish.

Stir-fries are among the ultimate stove-top go-tos. With just a wok or large skillet, you can combine thinly sliced meat or tofu with crisp vegetables and a flavorful sauce — soy, garlic, sesame oil, and a touch of honey or chili sauce work wonders. Serve it over rice or noodles, or even toss everything together in one pan for a complete, satisfying meal in minutes.

Pasta dishes also shine on the stove. A creamy garlic and spinach pasta, a zesty lemon-basil linguine, or a simple tomato-and-olive oil spaghetti can be whipped up with pantry staples and just one pot. Cooking the pasta directly in a flavorful broth or sauce (rather than water) intensifies the taste and saves you time and cleanup. Bonus: it also creates a naturally creamy texture thanks to the starch released from the pasta.

Eggs, often overlooked as a main ingredient, are another stove-top powerhouse. Think beyond breakfast — a shakshuka with poached eggs in spicy tomato sauce, a veggie-packed frittata, or a quick egg-fried rice can easily stand in as a satisfying lunch or dinner. Add a salad or some toasted bread, and you've got a complete meal with minimal effort.

Don't underestimate the simplicity of skillet meals either. One-pan stove-top recipes like sautéed chicken with lemon and capers, pan-seared salmon with garlic butter, or blackened shrimp tacos are restaurant-worthy meals that take less time than a delivery order. A hot pan, a few quality ingredients, and a splash of something acidic or creamy for finishing can turn a few fridge staples into something memorable.

What makes stove-top cooking so appealing — especially for busy lifestyles — is its immediacy. You're in control the entire time, adjusting heat, seasoning, and timing in real-time. There's no waiting for an oven to preheat or a slow cooker to finish. It's hands-on, intuitive, and rewarding — the kind of cooking that makes you feel both productive and creative in a short amount of time.

Best of all, these dishes are easy to scale, customize, and repeat. Once you find your favorite base recipes — a go-to stir-fry, a simple skillet pasta, a comforting rice bowl — you can switch out ingredients based on what's in season or what you have on hand. The possibilities are endless, and the reward is always the same: a hot, homemade meal made with love and very little time.

So when life gets busy and hunger strikes, head to the stove. With a few staples and a hot pan, your next favorite meal is just minutes away.

30-Minute Meals

When time is tight but your appetite (and standards) are high, 30-minute meals step in as your kitchen lifesaver. These dishes are designed for real life — quick enough to make between work and evening plans, yet flavorful and fulfilling enough to feel like something special. In just half an hour or less, you can prepare meals that are vibrant, nourishing, and far more satisfying than anything coming out of a takeout container. 30-Minute Meals prove that fast doesn't mean boring — and weeknight dinners don't have to be a compromise.

What sets these meals apart is efficiency — not just in cooking time, but in preparation and cleanup. It's about choosing ingredients that cook quickly, layering flavors strategically, and using simple techniques that get maximum results with minimum effort. You'll find plenty of recipes where chopping is minimal, cooking is mostly hands-off, and the whole process flows like a well-rehearsed dance.

Protein-packed mains like shrimp stir-fry, lemon-herb grilled chicken, or a skillet-seared steak with garlic butter can all come together in 20–25 minutes. Pair them with a pre-cooked grain, quick-cooking pasta, or a crunchy side salad and you've got a balanced, complete meal. Fish is especially great for fast meals — salmon, cod, or tilapia fillets cook in minutes and take beautifully to bold seasonings like paprika, citrus, miso, or chili-lime rubs.

Pasta dishes are also a 30-minute staple. Whether you're tossing spaghetti with olive oil, garlic, and red pepper flakes or making a creamy mushroom and spinach penne, pasta lends itself beautifully to fast, flavor-packed cooking. Use a single pot where possible, and reserve some pasta water to help emulsify sauces and bring everything together smoothly.

Vegetarian and plant-based meals are equally quick and versatile. Sautéed veggie tacos, chickpea curry, quinoa-stuffed peppers, or a colorful grain bowl with avocado, beans, and roasted veggies are all meals that deliver flavor, fiber, and satisfaction without needing hours on the stove. Many of these recipes benefit from pantry staples — canned beans, quick-cooking grains, frozen vegetables — making them even more convenient for weeknight use.

Another great time-saver? Prep-ahead elements. Cook a batch of grains or chop vegetables the night before, marinate proteins in the morning, or have dressings and sauces ready to go in the fridge. These small steps cut down cooking time significantly and make it easier to get dinner on the table — even when the day's been hectic.

And don't forget about one-pan or sheet pan meals — throw protein and vegetables onto a tray with oil and seasoning, roast for 25 minutes, and you've got a fuss-free dinner with only one pan to clean. Think honey-garlic chicken with broccoli, lemon-garlic shrimp with asparagus, or spicy tofu with bell peppers and sesame seeds.

The beauty of 30-minute meals isn't just in the speed — it's in the rhythm they create. They allow you to cook more often, try new things, and eat healthier without dreading the process. They give you back your evening while still letting you savor the simple pleasure of a home-cooked meal.

So if your evenings feel rushed or you think good food takes too long, think again. With the right ingredients, a little prep, and a solid game plan, your next delicious meal is just 30 minutes away.

Mix & Match Dinner Combos

Dinner doesn't have to be complicated to be delicious. In fact, some of the best meals come together when you stop following rules and start mixing and matching. Mix & Match Dinner Combos are all about freedom — the ability to pair ingredients based on what you have, what you love, and what your day calls for. Whether you're planning meals for the week or trying to use up leftovers, this flexible approach keeps things fun, flavorful, and stress-free.

Think of your dinner plate as a simple equation: one base + one protein + one veggie + one sauce or seasoning = a satisfying meal. Once you start thinking in this way, the combinations become endless. Start with a base — grains like rice, quinoa, couscous, or pasta; greens like spinach, arugula, or kale; or even roasted vegetables like cauliflower or sweet potatoes. These hearty components form the canvas of your plate.

Next, layer on your protein. This can be grilled chicken, seared tofu, roasted chickpeas, shrimp, or a boiled egg — whatever suits your appetite and lifestyle. You don't have to overthink it. Keeping a few cooked proteins in the fridge or freezer makes this step fast and easy, and lets you rotate flavors throughout the week without repeating meals.

Then come the vegetables — raw, roasted, steamed, pickled, or stir-fried. A handful of crunchy slaw, roasted Brussels sprouts, charred bell peppers, or juicy tomatoes brings color and freshness to your dish. You can also toss in whatever's seasonal or left in your crisper drawer — a great way to reduce waste while keeping meals interesting.

The final layer is where the magic happens: sauces, dressings, spices, or garnishes that tie everything together. A tahini lemon drizzle, chimichurri, teriyaki glaze, or herbed yogurt dressing can completely change the personality of a meal. Don't underestimate a squeeze of citrus, a dash of hot sauce, or a sprinkle of nuts or seeds —

these finishing touches often make the difference between "fine" and "fantastic."

What makes mix & match dinners so satisfying is the ability to tailor each plate to your mood, dietary needs, or time constraints. Craving something fresh and light? Try quinoa + grilled tofu + cucumber and radish + sesame-ginger dressing. Need comfort? Go for mashed potatoes + pan-seared chicken + sautéed greens + garlic butter sauce. Feeding a family with mixed preferences? Lay everything out buffet-style and let everyone build their own plates.

This method also works beautifully for batch cooking and meal prep. Cook a few grains and proteins on Sunday, prep a variety of veggies, and keep a few sauces or dressings in jars. Each night, you can mix and match to create something new without starting from scratch. It cuts down on decision fatigue while still letting you enjoy variety — a win-win in any busy household.

Mix & match meals also encourage mindful eating. When you build your plate piece by piece, you become more aware of what you're choosing and how each element contributes to the whole. It's a great way to practice balance — in nutrition, in flavor, and in life.

So forget rigid meal plans or fancy recipes for a moment. Open your fridge, get a little creative, and start building your own dinner combos. With this approach, every night can feel like something new — simple, flexible, and full of flavor.

Chapter 7
From the Oven – Bakes, Roasts & Gratins

There's something magical about the oven. It takes humble ingredients and transforms them into golden, bubbling, flavor-packed dishes with minimal effort. In this chapter, we celebrate the slow heat and comforting aroma of oven-cooked meals — from crisp roasts and cozy casseroles to creamy gratins and wholesome baked mains.

These are the kinds of dishes that fill your kitchen with warmth and your home with the smell of something wonderful in the making. Perfect for chilly evenings, weekend meals, or when you just want to let the oven do the heavy lifting, baked meals offer both flavor and convenience.

You'll discover everything from cheesy vegetable gratins and roasted meats with caramelized edges to layered casseroles and stuffed baked veggies. With smart prep and simple seasoning, these recipes are approachable yet deeply satisfying. They're ideal for feeding a crowd or cooking once and enjoying leftovers throughout the week.

We'll also guide you through the basics of oven cooking — how to roast to perfection, layer flavors in a bake, and achieve that irresistible golden crust on top. Whether you're baking a bubbling lasagna or roasting root vegetables with herbs, this chapter is your gateway to delicious oven-made comfort.

Casseroles & Comfort Bakes

There's a certain kind of magic that happens when ingredients come together in a single dish, bake slowly in the oven, and emerge bubbling, golden, and irresistible. Casseroles & Comfort Bakes are the very definition of home cooking — warm, hearty, and made to share. Whether it's a cheesy pasta bake, a creamy potato gratin, or a vegetable-stuffed lasagna, these dishes evoke the kind of comfort that only oven-baked meals can deliver.

Casseroles aren't just about nostalgia; they're about practicality too. They're ideal for feeding a crowd, make-ahead meal prepping, or simply stretching ingredients into something that feels like a feast. With just one baking dish, you can create layers of flavor, texture, and satisfaction — all while keeping cleanup minimal.

The structure of a great casserole is beautifully simple. You start with a hearty base — pasta, rice, potatoes, or even bread. Next, you build in your vegetables and protein: roasted veggies, sautéed mushrooms, pulled chicken, beans, or ground meat. Then comes the binder — often a creamy sauce, broth, or cheese-based mixture that brings it all together. Finally, the topping: a layer of melted cheese, crispy breadcrumbs, or crushed crackers to add texture and indulgence.

Take the classic baked mac and cheese — comforting, familiar, and endlessly adaptable. Add spinach, roasted garlic, or caramelized onions for a gourmet twist. Swap in cauliflower for half the pasta or add a spoonful of Dijon mustard to the cheese sauce for a sharper bite. Or try a vegetarian enchilada bake layered with tortillas, beans, roasted peppers, and a rich tomato-chili sauce — spicy, saucy, and utterly satisfying.

Comfort bakes also span global flavors. A shepherd's pie with a mashed potato topping and savory filling of ground lamb and vegetables is a British classic. Greek moussaka brings together layers of eggplant, spiced meat, and creamy béchamel. An Italian eggplant parmesan — with breaded slices baked in marinara and mozzarella — brings crispy edges and gooey centers in every bite.

Don't overlook breakfast and brunch bakes, either. Strata, made from cubes of bread, eggs, cheese, and vegetables, is perfect for mornings or meal prep. Savory bread puddings, frittata bakes, or even oatmeal casseroles can be prepped ahead and warmed for easy weekday meals.

The true charm of casseroles is how easily they adapt to what you have on hand. Leftover roasted vegetables, cooked meats, or even last night's rice can be transformed into a whole new dish with a few pantry staples and a little cheese. It's cooking that encourages creativity and reduces waste — all while delivering cozy satisfaction in every bite.

Best of all, casseroles are made for sharing. There's something about placing a hot dish in the center of the table, steam rising as it's served spoon by spoon, that brings people together. They're the kind of meals that feel generous and heartfelt, perfect for family dinners, potlucks, or quiet evenings when you just need a little edible comfort.

So preheat your oven, reach for your favorite baking dish, and fill your kitchen with the warmth of casseroles and comfort bakes. These are the meals that say, "Welcome home," even before you take the first bite.

Roasted Vegetables & Sides

There's something truly magical about roasting. With just a bit of oil, seasoning, and time in a hot oven, humble vegetables are transformed into caramelized, golden bites that burst with flavor. Roasted Vegetables & Sides are more than just supporting players on the plate — they often steal the show with their simplicity and depth. Whether served as an accompaniment or as part of a main dish, roasted veggies bring warmth, color, and texture to any meal.

Roasting concentrates natural sugars, adds a slight crispness to the edges, and creates that satisfying contrast between tender insides and toasty exteriors. Root vegetables are a classic go-to — think carrots, sweet potatoes, beets, and parsnips. When roasted, they develop a rich, earthy sweetness that's both rustic and refined. A simple drizzle of olive oil, a sprinkle of sea salt, and a few sprigs of fresh thyme or rosemary are often all you need to bring out their best.

But it's not just roots that shine in the oven. Cruciferous vegetables like Brussels sprouts, broccoli, and cauliflower become nutty and flavorful when roasted at high heat. Add a squeeze of lemon or a sprinkle of Parmesan cheese just before serving for a bright, savory finish. Even unexpected vegetables like cabbage wedges, green beans, or radishes take on a new personality in the oven — deeply satisfying and full of character.

The beauty of roasted vegetables is in their versatility. You can keep things classic with olive oil and herbs, or mix it up with spices from around the world. A dash of cumin and coriander gives a Middle Eastern vibe, while smoked paprika and chili flakes bring heat and depth. Tossing vegetables in a bit of balsamic vinegar or maple syrup before roasting adds a subtle sweetness and glossy finish that pairs beautifully with meats, grains, or cheeses.

Roasted sides also extend far beyond vegetables. Think about roasted garlic bread with herbs, crispy polenta fries, spiced chickpeas, or even baked apple slices with a pinch of cinnamon for a sweet-savory edge. Roasting isn't just a technique — it's a mindset, one that celebrates simplicity and patience, allowing the oven to do most of the work while you prepare the rest of your meal (or pour a glass of wine and relax).

One of the best parts of roasting is the ease of batch cooking. Fill a tray with a medley of vegetables, roast them all at once, and use them throughout the week. They reheat well, and they're easy to toss into salads, grain bowls, sandwiches, or soups. Leftover roasted vegetables also make a fantastic base for pureed dips or spreads — just blend with olive oil, lemon, and seasoning for an instant, flavorful snack.

And let's talk about presentation. Roasted vegetables are naturally beautiful — vibrant, golden, slightly charred — and they plate up like a dream. Whether served family-style in a big dish or artfully arranged beside your main, they add a touch of rustic charm to the table that feels both wholesome and indulgent.

In the end, roasted vegetables and sides are about celebrating what's simple and good. They take everyday ingredients and elevate them through heat, time, and care. They remind us that cooking doesn't have to be complicated to be absolutely delicious. So fire up the oven, grab your favorite produce, and get ready to roast your way to rich, deeply satisfying flavors.

Baked Pasta & Stuffed Dishes

Few things say "comfort food" quite like baked pasta and stuffed dishes. These are the meals that make your kitchen smell like home, that invite second helpings, and that somehow taste even better the next day. Baked Pasta & Stuffed Dishes are all about layers — of flavor, texture, and satisfaction. They're the kind of meals you crave when the weather cools down, when family comes over, or when you simply want something hearty, warm, and soul-soothing.

Baked pasta is the quintessential oven delight. From the bubbling cheese to the slightly crisp edges where the noodles meet the pan, there's nothing quite like digging into a freshly baked dish. Classic lasagna is, of course, the showstopper — alternating layers of pasta, rich meat or veggie filling, creamy béchamel or ricotta, and tomato sauce, all topped with golden, melted cheese. But the world of baked pasta goes far beyond lasagna. Think baked ziti with marinara and mozzarella, creamy mac and cheese with a crispy breadcrumb topping, or rigatoni al forno layered with sausage, spinach, and béchamel for a restaurant-worthy twist.

What makes these dishes special is how they combine comfort with structure. Everything is assembled, baked, and served in one dish — which means less mess, easier cleanup, and leftovers that reheat beautifully. They're ideal for meal prep, potlucks, or feeding a family with minimal stress. Once in the oven, the hard part is done — all that's left is the anticipation of that first melty bite.

Stuffed dishes offer the same kind of comfort, but with a playful, presentation-forward twist. Vegetables like bell peppers, zucchini, eggplant, tomatoes, and even mushrooms become edible vessels for delicious fillings. You can stuff them with seasoned rice, quinoa, or couscous mixed with herbs, cheese, beans, or ground meat. Once baked, the veggies become tender and sweet, and the filling soaks up all their juices — a perfect balance of flavor and texture.

Stuffed shells and manicotti are another baked favorite. Large pasta shells are filled with ricotta, spinach, or even a bold meat mixture, nestled into a baking dish with rich tomato or cream sauce, and finished with a generous layer of bubbling cheese. It's a dish that always feels like it took more effort than it did — impressive, indulgent, and deeply satisfying.

The best part? These dishes are endlessly customizable. Vegetarian? Use roasted vegetables, lentils, or mushrooms. Gluten-free? Choose rice pasta or stuff sweet potatoes instead of shells. Love bold flavors? Add pesto, spicy sausage, sun-dried tomatoes, or smoked paprika to your fillings. They're made for adapting to your taste, your pantry, and your cravings.

Even better, both baked pasta and stuffed dishes are perfect for make-ahead cooking. Assemble your dish in the morning (or the night before), refrigerate it, and bake when you're ready. Not only does this save time, but letting the ingredients sit also allows the flavors to meld, resulting in an even richer taste.

In a fast-paced world, these oven-made meals invite you to slow down, gather around the table, and savor something made with care. Whether you're feeding a crowd, stocking your freezer, or just treating yourself to something warm and satisfying, baked pasta and stuffed dishes are comfort food at its very best — generous, gooey, and guaranteed to please.

Sheet Pan Magic

There's something truly magical about tossing a few ingredients onto a sheet pan, sliding it into the oven, and pulling out a full meal that's flavorful, perfectly cooked, and beautifully golden — with just one pan to clean. Sheet Pan Magic is more than a kitchen shortcut; it's a way to simplify dinnertime without sacrificing quality, texture, or taste. Whether you're cooking for one, feeding a family, or prepping for the week, sheet pan meals offer a delicious blend of convenience and creativity.

The beauty of the sheet pan lies in its simplicity. It's a wide, flat canvas that lets you roast proteins and vegetables side by side, allowing them to mingle, caramelize, and absorb each other's flavors. It's a method that rewards minimal effort with maximum payoff. With just a little chopping, seasoning, and arranging, dinner practically makes itself — no boiling, no stirring, and no sink full of pots and pans to scrub afterward.

One of the keys to sheet pan success is choosing ingredients that cook at similar rates or staggering the cooking time. Root vegetables like potatoes, carrots, and sweet potatoes take longer to roast, so they might go in first. Quicker-cooking ingredients like zucchini, bell peppers, asparagus, or fish can be added later. By understanding your ingredients' timing, you'll achieve that perfect balance of tender insides and crisp, caramelized edges.

Proteins like chicken thighs, salmon fillets, shrimp, or tofu thrive on a sheet pan. Chicken becomes golden and juicy, shrimp gets a delicate char, and tofu turns crispy with a simple toss in oil and seasoning. Pair them with vegetables, and you've got a one-pan dinner that's as colorful as it is complete. Want to boost it even further? Toss in some cherry tomatoes, olives, or lemon slices for pops of brightness and acidity.

Sheet pan meals also lend themselves well to global flavors. Go Mediterranean with oregano, garlic, and a drizzle of olive oil. Try Asian-inspired blends with soy sauce, sesame oil, and ginger. Or spice it up with Middle Eastern za'atar, cumin, and sumac. Because everything roasts together, even the simplest seasoning mix has time to deepen and develop, infusing the entire dish with layered flavor.

And it's not just dinners that benefit from this method. Sheet pan breakfasts — like roasted veggie and egg bakes or baked hash browns with sausage — are perfect for weekends or prepping ahead. You can even make desserts like baked fruit with cinnamon and honey or toasty granola clusters on the same humble tray.

Cleanup is as magical as the cooking. A sheet of parchment paper or foil makes washing up almost nonexistent, and with just one pan, your kitchen stays tidy and efficient. It's an ideal solution for busy weeknights, lazy Sundays, or any time you want to cook without the chaos.

Sheet pan cooking invites creativity. It's a blank slate for trying new ingredients, exploring different spice blends, and using up what's already in your fridge. It's about ease, yes — but also about flavor, color, and smart cooking that makes life more delicious.

So embrace the magic. Grab a pan, preheat your oven, and discover just how rewarding it can be to toss, roast, and serve a complete, satisfying meal with minimal effort and maximum joy.

Chapter 8
Around the World on a Plate – Global Inspiration

Food is a universal language — one that tells stories of culture, tradition, and the joy of sharing. In this chapter, we journey across continents and cuisines to bring you globally inspired dishes that transport your taste buds without leaving your kitchen. Whether it's the bold spices of India, the fresh herbs of the Mediterranean, or the savory-sweet balance of Asian flavors, each recipe is a celebration of culinary diversity.

Exploring international recipes doesn't have to be intimidating. These dishes are simplified without compromising authenticity, making it easy for home cooks to experiment with new ingredients, techniques, and flavor combinations. From tacos and curries to stir-fries, shawarma, and pasta — you'll discover meals that are both approachable and exciting.

Cooking global cuisine also opens the door to new pantry staples — like miso, harissa, tamari, or couscous — that can become everyday essentials in your kitchen. We'll guide you on how to substitute ingredients if needed and adapt recipes to your personal preferences.

This chapter is all about adventure and connection — finding new favorites, revisiting childhood flavors, or experiencing a taste of places you dream of visiting. So grab your passport (and your spatula) — it's time to explore the world, one delicious dish at a time.

Asian Delights: Stir-Fries & Dumplings

When it comes to bold flavors, quick cooking, and unbeatable satisfaction, few meals deliver like a good stir-fry or a plate of perfectly steamed dumplings. Asian Delights: Stir-Fries & Dumplings is all about capturing the heart of Asian home cooking — where speed meets flavor, and where simple ingredients transform into something absolutely crave-worthy.

Stir-fries are the weeknight hero of many Asian kitchens. With a sizzling hot pan, fresh ingredients, and just a few minutes, you can create dishes that are full of texture, color, and depth. The key is high heat and constant movement — cooking quickly so that vegetables stay crisp, proteins remain tender, and sauces cling beautifully to each bite. It's a dance of flavor and motion, where every element has its moment in the wok.

Start with aromatics like garlic, ginger, scallions, or shallots. As they hit the pan, they release intense fragrance — the perfect base for building your stir-fry. Next, thinly sliced proteins like chicken, beef, shrimp, or tofu go in, searing quickly for maximum flavor. Then come the vegetables: broccoli, bell peppers, snow peas, mushrooms, bok choy — anything fresh, colorful, and quick-cooking works wonderfully.

The sauce is where the magic happens. Soy sauce, oyster sauce, hoisin, sesame oil, rice vinegar, or chili paste — any combination can work depending on the flavor profile you're after. For a classic savory stir-fry, mix soy sauce, garlic, and a bit of brown sugar. Want something spicy and tangy? Add sambal or sriracha with lime juice and honey. A touch of cornstarch in the sauce helps it thicken slightly, so it coats every bite with glossy perfection.

Pair your stir-fry with jasmine rice, brown rice, or noodles, and you've got a meal that's fast, fresh, and deeply satisfying — ready in under 20 minutes, yet packed with character.

And then there are dumplings — delicate pockets of joy, filled with savory goodness and wrapped with care. Dumplings hold a special place in Asian culinary traditions, symbolizing wealth, family, and celebration. Whether boiled, steamed, or pan-fried, these small but mighty bites are always a hit.

Making dumplings at home is surprisingly fun and meditative. Store-bought wrappers make the process accessible, and fillings can be as classic or creative as you like. Pork and cabbage with ginger and soy? Timeless. Shrimp and chive with sesame oil? Elegant. Mushroom and tofu with hoisin and scallion? A flavorful vegetarian twist. The key is to mix your filling well, keep it moist but not watery, and seal the edges with care.

Pan-frying gives you the best of both worlds — a crispy base and a tender, juicy top. Steam them for a soft, pillowy texture, or boil for a lighter finish. Don't forget a dipping sauce: a mix of soy sauce, rice vinegar, chili oil, and a touch of garlic adds zing and balance.

Stir-fries and dumplings offer more than just delicious food — they offer connection. They bring people together, whether gathered around the stove for a quick dinner or sitting at the table folding dumplings by hand. These dishes are joyful, hands-on, and full of life, inviting you to explore, customize, and savor every bite.

So grab your wok, roll up your sleeves, and dive into the sizzling, savory world of Asian delights. From crisp stir-fries to tender dumplings, these dishes are made to be loved — again and again.

Mediterranean Magic: Mezze & Mains

There's a reason Mediterranean cuisine is beloved around the world — it's colorful, fresh, bursting with flavor, and rooted in the joy of sharing. Mediterranean Magic: Mezze & Mains celebrates the vibrant traditions of coastal kitchens from Greece to Lebanon, Italy to Turkey. With simple ingredients, bold spices, and a focus on balance and variety, this region's food culture invites you to slow down, savor, and nourish both body and soul.

Let's start with mezze — the Mediterranean answer to tapas. Mezze isn't just a collection of appetizers; it's an entire experience built around small plates meant for sharing. It encourages conversation, community, and a variety of flavors in one meal. Think of it as a vibrant spread of dips, bites, and nibbles — each dish offering a different texture and taste, yet harmonizing together on the table.

At the heart of any mezze platter are iconic dips like hummus — creamy chickpeas blended with tahini, lemon, and garlic — and baba ganoush, made from smoky roasted eggplant. These are usually served with warm pita or flatbread, perfect for scooping and layering flavors. Tzatziki, a refreshing cucumber-yogurt dip with dill and garlic, adds a cool contrast, while muhammara, a blend of roasted red peppers, walnuts, and pomegranate molasses, brings a tangy, slightly spicy note.

To complement the dips, mezze often includes stuffed grape leaves (dolmas), falafel, olives, feta, and roasted or pickled vegetables. There's a rhythm to the variety — crunchy, creamy, tangy, herby — making it feel like a feast even before the main course arrives.

When it comes to mains, Mediterranean cooking is equally generous and vibrant. Dishes often feature lean proteins like grilled chicken, lamb, or seafood, roasted vegetables, and wholesome grains like bulgur or couscous. What ties it all together are bold seasonings — think oregano, cumin, coriander, mint, and za'atar — plus the liberal use of olive oil, lemon, and garlic, which bring both brightness and richness.

A classic Greek moussaka, with layers of eggplant, spiced meat, and creamy béchamel, is a comforting bake perfect for family meals. Lebanese chicken tawook, marinated in yogurt, garlic, and lemon, is delicious grilled and served with garlicky toum or fresh tabbouleh. From Italy, dishes like chicken piccata, pasta primavera, or a simple grilled fish drizzled with lemon and herbs showcase the lighter, cleaner side of the Mediterranean palette.

Plant-based eaters will also find plenty of inspiration here — dishes like roasted eggplant with tahini, chickpea and spinach stew, couscous bowls with grilled veggies, or stuffed bell peppers with herbed rice offer all the richness of flavor without relying on meat or dairy.

What makes Mediterranean food so magical is its harmony — the way fresh ingredients, bold herbs, and a balance of textures all come together on one plate (or across many). It's food that feels good to eat — both physically and emotionally — and that naturally brings people together around the table.

So embrace the mezze mindset. Pile up your plate with variety, drizzle on the olive oil, sprinkle that feta, and pass the bread. With every bite of this sun-drenched cuisine, you'll be reminded that cooking — and eating — is meant to be a celebration.

Latin Flavors: Tacos, Rice, and Beans

Latin American cuisine is a joyful celebration of bold spices, bright colors, and comforting traditions. At its heart, it's about food that brings people together — full of soul, flavor, and warmth. Latin Flavors: Tacos, Rice, and Beans dives into some of the most iconic and beloved staples of Latin cooking. Whether you're making a weeknight taco spread, simmering a pot of seasoned beans, or preparing a fragrant rice dish, these meals are as satisfying as they are versatile.

Let's begin with tacos — the ultimate handheld food. Tacos are far more than just meat in a tortilla; they're an entire world of flavor combinations, textures, and regional styles. From Mexico's street-style al pastor and carne asada to coastal fish tacos or slow-braised birria, there's no wrong way to taco. Start with warm corn or flour tortillas, then layer with your choice of grilled, stewed, or roasted protein, top with salsas, pickled onions, fresh cilantro, and a squeeze of lime. The real beauty of tacos lies in the toppings — spicy, fresh, crunchy, and tangy elements that turn every bite into a flavor explosion.

And don't forget about vegetarian tacos. Grilled mushrooms, crispy chickpeas, sautéed peppers and onions, or roasted sweet potatoes with cumin and chili powder are all delicious plant-based options. Add avocado slices, a drizzle of crema or lime-spiked yogurt, and a sprinkle of cotija cheese, and you've got a taco that holds its own against any meat version.

Now, let's talk about rice and beans — the heart and soul of Latin comfort food. This humble duo shows up in almost every country, with each region adding its own spin. In Cuba, you'll find moros y cristianos, a savory mix of black beans and white rice cooked together with garlic, onion, and bay leaf. In Puerto Rico and the Dominican Republic, arroz con gandules (rice with pigeon peas) is often flavored with sofrito — a blend of peppers, garlic, onion, and herbs that forms the aromatic base of many dishes.

Mexican-style rice, often tinged red with tomato and laced with garlic and cumin, pairs perfectly with black or pinto beans that have been simmered with onion, bay leaf, and just a hint of smoky spice. For a more indulgent version, try refried beans — smooth, creamy, and often cooked with a little oil or butter for richness. These aren't just side dishes; they're meals in themselves.

One of the best things about rice and beans is their ability to stretch ingredients. They're affordable, filling, and protein-packed, especially when served with grilled meat, fish, or vegetables. Add a fried egg, avocado slices, or plantains on the side, and you've got a complete meal full of flavor and balance.

Latin cooking also invites customization and creativity. Whether you're building a taco bar, prepping burrito bowls, or serving rice and beans with grilled chicken, the components can be made ahead of time and combined in countless ways. It's the kind of food that's generous, adaptable, and always full of life.

So fire up the skillet, warm your tortillas, and don't hold back on the lime and salsa. From tacos to rice and beans, these Latin flavors bring sunshine to the plate and a whole lot of joy to the table.

European Comforts: Pastas & Pies

When we think of comfort food, our minds often wander to the charming kitchens of Europe — where hearty pastas simmer in rich sauces and golden pies emerge from warm ovens, filling the room with irresistible aromas. European Comforts: Pastas & Pies is all about embracing the kind of food that soothes the soul and satisfies every craving. These dishes carry generations of tradition and celebrate simple ingredients transformed through love, patience, and a touch of indulgence.

Let's start with pastas, the beating heart of Italian home cooking and a staple throughout much of Europe. Whether it's a humble spaghetti aglio e olio or a decadent fettuccine alfredo, pasta is a blank canvas that welcomes a world of flavor. Classic dishes like lasagna, layered with meat, béchamel, and marinara, or pasta alla vodka, silky with cream and tomato, are pure comfort in a bowl. Even simpler recipes — like buttered noodles with grated Parmesan and cracked black pepper — offer a kind of nostalgic joy that's hard to beat.

European pasta dishes are more than just sauce and noodles; they're about balance and richness. Carbonara, with its blend of eggs, cheese, and pancetta, offers a creamy bite without a drop of cream. Puttanesca, sharp with capers, olives, and garlic, brings bold flavor with minimal ingredients. And across the continent, variations abound — from German spaetzle served with butter and herbs to Hungarian túrós csusza, a cottage cheese noodle dish often finished with crispy bacon.

But comfort doesn't end at the stovetop — it continues into the oven, where savory pies have long been a staple of European cuisine. These golden, flaky creations are everything we crave when the weather cools or when we want something hearty and satisfying.

Take British cottage pie, for instance — a savory meat filling topped with a smooth layer of mashed potatoes, baked until golden and bubbling. Or its cousin, shepherd's pie, traditionally made with lamb and aromatic vegetables, creating a perfect blend of textures and flavors. Both are ideal for making ahead and reheating, which only seems to deepen their flavor.

In France, you'll find quiches, like the famous quiche Lorraine, where creamy custard, cheese, and bacon bake inside a delicate pastry crust. These egg-based pies are deceptively simple and incredibly versatile, welcoming everything from spinach and mushrooms to goat cheese and roasted tomatoes.

Elsewhere in Europe, you'll find rustic favorites like Greek spanakopita, with its layers of flaky phyllo dough and a savory spinach-feta filling, or Italian torta rustica, stuffed with cured meats, cheeses, and greens. These pies are as beautiful to look at as they are satisfying to eat — perfect for sharing at gatherings or enjoying as leftovers throughout the week.

What ties these pastas and pies together is the sense of home and heritage they evoke. They remind us of slow dinners with family, passed-down recipes, and the comforting rhythm of cooking something from scratch. They also allow for flexibility — adapt them with seasonal vegetables, different cheeses, or plant-based proteins, and they'll still offer the same warmth and flavor.

So whether you're simmering a big pot of pasta or pulling a golden pie from the oven, embrace the comfort and charm of Europe's most beloved dishes. They're simple, soulful, and always worth every bite.

Chapter 9
Sweet Treats – Desserts to Crave

Dessert is more than just the end of a meal — it's a moment of joy, a reward, and sometimes, a little escape. In this chapter, we dive into the irresistible world of sweet treats, where every recipe is designed to delight the senses and satisfy those sugar cravings with love and creativity.

Whether you're in the mood for rich chocolate indulgence, fruity freshness, or something light and creamy, you'll find a variety of desserts to suit every taste and occasion. From classic cookies and decadent cakes to no-bake bites and quick puddings, these recipes are both comforting and impressive — perfect for everyday enjoyment or special celebrations.

Don't worry if you're not an experienced baker — we've kept things simple and approachable. You'll find easy-to-follow instructions, baking tips, and helpful tricks to avoid common mistakes. You'll also learn how to personalize your sweets with toppings, sauces, and seasonal twists.

Dessert is also a beautiful way to share love. A warm pie served at a family gathering, a tray of cookies made with kids, or a perfectly chilled mousse on a romantic evening — these are the moments where sweetness becomes a memory.

So grab your mixing bowl, preheat the oven (or not!), and let your sweet side shine. Because life's too short not to enjoy dessert.

Cakes, Cupcakes & Loaves

There's something universally comforting about the smell of cake baking in the oven — that warm, sweet aroma that fills your kitchen and promises something special at the end of it. Cakes, Cupcakes & Loaves are more than just desserts; they're expressions of love, celebration, and everyday joy. Whether you're baking a rich chocolate cake for a birthday, whipping up a tray of cupcakes for a school event, or making a simple banana loaf to enjoy with tea, these treats have a way of bringing people together and creating lasting memories.

Let's start with cakes — the grand centerpieces of dessert tables. From fluffy sponge cakes to dense flourless varieties, cake is a canvas for creativity. A classic vanilla layer cake with whipped buttercream never fails to impress, while a chocolate fudge cake satisfies even the deepest cravings. Want to elevate things? Add espresso, fruit preserves, or spiced ganache between layers, or infuse the batter with citrus zest or floral notes like rosewater or lavender.

One of the best things about cakes is their adaptability. With just a few pantry staples — flour, eggs, sugar, and butter — you can create endless variations. Swap in almond flour for a nutty twist, or use yogurt or sour cream to keep things extra moist. Cakes can be celebratory or simple, elaborate or rustic. Whether it's a towering layer cake or a humble single-pan bake with a dusting of powdered sugar, the charm is always there.

Then come cupcakes, the miniature marvels of the baking world. These little treats deliver all the satisfaction of a full-sized cake in a perfectly portioned bite. Cupcakes are fun, versatile, and a hit with all ages. From red velvet with cream cheese frosting to lemon poppyseed with a citrus glaze, there's a flavor to suit every mood and season.

The magic of cupcakes lies in the decorating. Whether swirled with buttercream roses or topped with sprinkles and ganache, they're as delightful to look at as they are to eat. They're also great for parties and gatherings, easy to transport, and a dream for anyone who loves a little creativity in the kitchen. Bonus: they bake faster than full-sized cakes, so they're perfect for last-minute sweet cravings or spontaneous baking projects.

And then there are loaves — the understated stars of the baking world. Think banana bread, zucchini loaf, lemon drizzle cake, or a spiced pumpkin loaf with crunchy streusel topping. These bakes are perfect for breakfast, snack time, or a cozy afternoon pick-me-up. They're often lower fuss than layered cakes or cupcakes, requiring just one pan and a quick mix before baking.

Loaf cakes shine when made with seasonal ingredients. In summer, try blueberry or peach loaves with a hint of almond. In fall and winter, warm spices like cinnamon, nutmeg, and ginger pair beautifully with apples, pears, or squash. You can also make them healthier with whole wheat flour, reduced sugar, or add-ins like chia seeds, oats, or flax.

No matter which direction you go — rich and decadent, light and fruity, classic or contemporary — baking cakes, cupcakes, and loaves brings joy to both the baker and the lucky ones who get to enjoy the final product. It's about slowing down, measuring with care, and savoring something made from scratch.

So preheat your oven, pull out your mixing bowls, and get ready to create something sweet, warm, and full of heart. Because in the world of baking, it's not just about the treat — it's about the moment you create along with it.

Pies, Tarts & Crisps

There's a timeless comfort in a dessert that's wrapped in a golden crust or bubbling under a blanket of sweet, buttery crumbs. Pies, Tarts & Crisps are the soul of home baking — rustic yet elegant, simple yet deeply satisfying. These are the kinds of desserts that connect us to our roots, our families, and the seasons, offering a slice of sweetness that feels both familiar and extraordinary.

Let's begin with pies, perhaps the most iconic of all. Whether you're serving a classic apple pie with a lattice crust or a rich, creamy chocolate silk pie, there's something magical about cutting into a golden shell and revealing the goodness inside. Fruit pies are especially beloved — peach, cherry, blueberry, mixed berry, or rhubarb — all capturing the essence of fresh produce at its peak. The filling bubbles up in the oven, the juices thicken into syrupy perfection, and the crust becomes flaky, crisp, and impossibly inviting.

Making pie dough from scratch might seem daunting, but it's simpler than it looks — just flour, butter, a pinch of salt, and ice water. The key is to keep everything cold and not to overwork the dough. Of course, there's no shame in using a store-bought crust when time is short. It's all about the comfort, after all.

Tarts bring a touch of refinement to the table. With their delicate, shallow crusts and often more elegant presentation, tarts can be either sweet or savory, but in this case, we're celebrating the sweet side. Think of a lemon tart with a silky curd and golden shell, or a French fruit tart layered with vanilla pastry cream and glossy seasonal fruit. Rustic galettes, the freeform cousin of the tart, let you fold dough casually around your filling, creating a beautifully imperfect edge that looks just as good as it tastes.

Then there are crisps, the easiest and perhaps coziest of the bunch. No rolling or crimping required — just toss your fruit with a little sugar and cornstarch, layer it in a baking dish, and cover it with a crumble topping made from oats, brown sugar, flour, butter, and maybe a sprinkle of cinnamon or chopped nuts. Pop it in the oven until the top is golden and the fruit is bubbling beneath. A scoop of vanilla ice cream on top? Absolute heaven.

What makes these desserts so universally loved is their seasonal flexibility. In summer, go for berry tarts or peach crisps. In autumn, apple pies and pear galettes shine. Winter is perfect for citrus tarts, pecan pies, or even frozen-fruit crisps. Spring offers the freshness of rhubarb, strawberry, and light custard-based fillings. You can adjust spices, swap flours, add herbs, or try unexpected ingredients like ginger, balsamic vinegar, or cardamom to give your desserts a signature twist.

Beyond flavor, these bakes bring something emotional to the table. Pies cool on windowsills, crisps are served warm straight from the oven, and tarts are displayed with pride at dinner parties. They're passed down in handwritten recipes, brought to potlucks and holidays, and enjoyed in quiet, everyday moments.

So roll out that dough, slice up some fruit, or whip up a buttery crumble topping. Whether you're making a showstopping tart or a weeknight crisp, these desserts promise more than sweetness — they offer comfort, care, and the joy of something made from scratch, by hand, and with heart.

Cookies & No-Bake Treats

There's a special kind of joy that comes from whipping up a batch of cookies or assembling an easy, no-bake treat. These are the little sweets that make a big impact — perfect for lunchbox surprises, after-dinner indulgence, or a cozy afternoon snack with a hot drink. Cookies & No-Bake Treats offer instant gratification, creative possibilities, and that nostalgic feeling of sneaking a treat straight from the cooling rack (or the fridge). Whether you're in the mood to bake or looking to skip the oven altogether, this is where delicious meets doable.

Let's start with cookies, the beloved classic that never goes out of style. From crispy-edged chocolate chip cookies to chewy oatmeal raisin or rich peanut butter, cookies are the kind of treat that's easy to love and even easier to share. A few basic pantry ingredients — flour, butter, sugar, eggs — are all you need to get started. And once you have a base recipe, the fun really begins. Add-ins like chopped nuts, dried fruits, coconut, espresso powder, or even a pinch of sea salt can transform a simple cookie into something completely unique.

Soft-baked cookies with gooey centers are perfect for cozy moments, while crisp biscotti or lace cookies are elegant enough to serve with tea or coffee. You can shape them by hand, roll them into balls, drop them by spoonfuls, or cut them into perfect rounds — every method adds its own charm. And for a festive twist, sandwich two cookies with frosting, jam, or ganache, or dip them in chocolate and add sprinkles for a fun, decorative finish.

If turning on the oven feels like too much effort — especially in warm weather or on busy days — that's where no-bake treats shine. These are the no-fuss desserts that come together with minimal tools and chill in the fridge or freezer instead of baking. They're fast, fun, and often involve little hands if you're baking with kids.

One of the most popular no-bake options is the classic chocolate oat cookie, made with cocoa, peanut butter, oats, and just a touch of butter and sugar. Scoop, drop, chill — and they're ready to enjoy. For something a little more refined, try energy bites made with dates, nuts, chia seeds, and dark chocolate chips. They're nutritious, satisfying, and incredibly versatile, working equally well as a dessert or on-the-go snack.

Another favorite? No-bake bars and slices. Think layered peanut butter and chocolate bars, lemon-coconut slices, or cheesecake bars made with a graham cracker crust and creamy filling. These bars are great for potlucks, picnics, or meal prep — they store well and serve easily in tidy squares or wedges.

Even something as simple as chocolate-covered pretzels, marshmallow clusters, or frozen yogurt bark counts as a no-bake treat. With a few pantry staples and a little imagination, you can turn ordinary ingredients into something special.

The best part of cookies and no-bake treats is the freedom they offer. You don't need to be a professional baker to make something sweet and satisfying. They're forgiving, fun, and endlessly customizable — which means there's always room to experiment and find your new favorite.

So whether you're preheating the oven or reaching for a mixing bowl and a fridge shelf, these little indulgences prove that homemade sweetness doesn't have to be complicated. Just a few ingredients, a little creativity, and a craving — that's all it takes to create a moment worth savoring.

Fruity Endings & Light Options

Not every dessert needs to be rich or decadent to feel like a satisfying finale. Sometimes, the perfect ending to a meal is something light, refreshing, and just sweet enough to leave you feeling content. Fruity Endings & Light Options celebrates those desserts that embrace natural sweetness, fresh flavors, and airy textures — perfect for warmer months, after a hearty dinner, or anytime you're craving something on the brighter side of indulgence.

Fruit-forward desserts have long been the go-to for simplicity and elegance. A perfectly ripe peach, a bowl of juicy berries, or a few slices of chilled melon can feel luxurious on their own. But when you elevate fruit with thoughtful pairings — a drizzle of honey, a dusting of cinnamon, a spoonful of yogurt, or a handful of toasted nuts — you turn the everyday into something extraordinary.

One of the easiest and most beautiful fruity desserts is a fruit salad, but not the kind tossed together as an afterthought. A truly great fruit salad is intentional — a mix of seasonal fruits like berries, citrus, mango, kiwi, or stone fruits, enhanced with herbs like mint or basil, and brought together with a zesty lime or orange-honey dressing. Add a touch of grated ginger, a few drops of rosewater, or a splash of balsamic reduction, and your fruit salad becomes something special.

Grilled fruit is another unexpected delight. Grilling peaches, pineapple, or figs intensifies their sweetness and adds a slight smokiness that pairs beautifully with a scoop of frozen yogurt or a spoonful of ricotta. Add a drizzle of maple syrup or a sprinkle of sea salt for contrast, and you've got a simple yet impressive dessert that comes together in minutes.

When you want something chilled and spoonable, fruit-based sorbets, parfaits, or yogurt bowls shine. Sorbets made with just fruit, water, and a touch of sweetener are a naturally dairy-free, gluten-free treat that bursts with real fruit flavor. Meanwhile, layering Greek yogurt with berries, granola, and a swirl of fruit compote creates a parfait that's equal parts dessert and breakfast. It's a refreshing choice that feels indulgent without being heavy.

Chia puddings, made with chia seeds soaked in almond milk or coconut milk and sweetened with a touch of honey or maple syrup, are another excellent light option. They're full of fiber and omega-3s, but most importantly, they're creamy, satisfying, and customizable. Top with tropical fruits, toasted coconut, or a dollop of fruit preserves for a fun and nutritious dessert.

For a more elegant twist, poached fruits like pears in spiced wine, apples in citrus syrup, or plums with vanilla and honey offer a warm, delicate way to enjoy dessert. Served with a spoonful of crème fraîche or a scoop of low-sugar vanilla ice cream, they strike a perfect balance between comfort and lightness.

The beauty of these fruity and light options lies not only in their fresh, vibrant taste but also in how they make you feel — nourished, satisfied, and never overly full. They're desserts that align with how many of us want to eat today: with balance, with joy, and with just the right amount of sweetness.

So when the moment calls for a gentle finish, turn to nature's candy and the lighter side of indulgence. Whether it's a chilled berry bowl, a grilled peach, or a spoonful of chia pudding, these treats remind us that dessert doesn't have to be heavy to be memorable — sometimes, it just has to be fresh.

Chapter 10
Plant-Powered Plates –
Vegetarian & Vegan Goodness

Dessert is more than just the end of a meal — it's a moment of joy, a reward, and sometimes, a little escape. In this chapter, we dive into the irresistible world of sweet treats, where every recipe is designed to delight the senses and satisfy those sugar cravings with love and creativity.

Whether you're in the mood for rich chocolate indulgence, fruity freshness, or something light and creamy, you'll find a variety of desserts to suit every taste and occasion. From classic cookies and decadent cakes to no-bake bites and quick puddings, these recipes are both comforting and impressive — perfect for everyday enjoyment or special celebrations.

Don't worry if you're not an experienced baker — we've kept things simple and approachable. You'll find easy-to-follow instructions, baking tips, and helpful tricks to avoid common mistakes. You'll also learn how to personalize your sweets with toppings, sauces, and seasonal twists.

Dessert is also a beautiful way to share love. A warm pie served at a family gathering, a tray of cookies made with kids, or a perfectly chilled mousse on a romantic evening — these are the moments where sweetness becomes a memory.

So grab your mixing bowl, preheat the oven (or not!), and let your sweet side shine. Because life's too short not to enjoy dessert.

Vibrant Veggie Mains

Gone are the days when vegetables played a supporting role on the plate. Today, they're front and center — bold, colorful, and bursting with flavor. Vibrant Veggie Mains is all about celebrating the magic that happens when vegetables take the spotlight, proving that plant-based meals can be just as hearty, satisfying, and crave-worthy as any meat dish. Whether you're a lifelong vegetarian, a plant-curious foodie, or simply looking to eat more greens, these dishes showcase the full spectrum of what vegetables can do.

The secret to making veggie mains feel substantial lies in how you layer flavor and texture. Roasted, grilled, sautéed, mashed, spiralized — each cooking method brings out a different personality in your produce. Combine that with global spices, fresh herbs, hearty grains, and proteins like legumes, nuts, or cheese, and you're well on your way to a meal that's nourishing and full of life.

Take the humble cauliflower — it transforms when roasted with olive oil, smoked paprika, and garlic. Pair it with tahini drizzle and crispy chickpeas over a bed of couscous, and suddenly you've got a Middle Eastern-inspired bowl bursting with flavor and texture. Or consider portobello mushrooms — when marinated and grilled, they become meaty and rich, perfect for stacking in burgers or slicing over polenta with a balsamic glaze.

Stuffed vegetables are another brilliant way to create filling veggie mains. Think bell peppers brimming with spiced lentils and rice, zucchini boats loaded with quinoa and feta, or eggplants baked with tomato sauce and melty mozzarella. These dishes feel cozy and comforting, and they're easy to adapt with whatever you have in your fridge or pantry.

Then there's the world of hearty veggie curries and stews. Sweet potatoes, spinach, peas, and carrots simmered in coconut milk with ginger and curry spices make for a bowl that's warming and deeply satisfying. Served with rice, naan, or even a fresh salad, it's a dish that brings comfort and nourishment in equal measure. Similarly, a robust ratatouille — with eggplant, tomatoes, zucchini, and bell peppers — is a celebration of Mediterranean abundance that pairs beautifully with crusty bread or pasta.

Bowls and platters also lend themselves beautifully to vibrant veggie meals. Build your own with roasted seasonal vegetables, hummus or pesto, a soft-boiled egg or grilled tofu, and a grain like farro, wild rice, or bulgur. Drizzle with a tangy vinaigrette, sprinkle with seeds or microgreens, and you've got a dish that's not only visually stunning but deeply satisfying.

Don't underestimate the power of a veggie pasta, either. A garlicky sauté of spinach, mushrooms, and cherry tomatoes tossed with linguine and a sprinkle of parmesan is simple, fast, and utterly delicious. Or go bold with a roasted butternut squash sauce blended with sage and a splash of cream — velvety, rich, and totally meatless.

What makes veggie mains so exciting is how adaptable and inclusive they are. They're great for every season, every skill level, and every dietary need. Whether you're craving something warm and hearty or light and fresh, vegetables have the range and richness to deliver.

So open your fridge, hit the farmer's market, or dig into your garden — and let your vegetables lead the way. With the right seasoning, creativity, and care, these vibrant veggie mains will not only nourish your body but also delight your senses and satisfy your soul.

Meatless Protein Options

When most people think about protein, their minds go straight to meat. But there's a whole world of meatless protein options that are not only nourishing and satisfying but also versatile, affordable, and absolutely delicious. Whether you're vegetarian, vegan, or simply looking to cut back on meat, these plant-based powerhouses prove that you don't have to compromise flavor or nutrition when going meatless.

Let's start with the stars of the meatless protein world: legumes. Beans, lentils, and chickpeas are staples in many global cuisines — and for good reason. They're packed with protein, fiber, and iron, and they take on flavor beautifully. Toss chickpeas into salads or roast them for a crunchy topping. Simmer black beans with garlic and cumin for taco fillings, or blend white beans into creamy dips. Lentils are especially versatile — brown or green lentils hold their shape well in soups and stews, while red lentils cook quickly and melt into curries and sauces.

Tofu and tempeh are next in line, offering complete proteins made from soybeans. Tofu, with its neutral flavor and range of textures (silken, soft, firm, extra firm), can be grilled, scrambled, baked, or blended. Press it to remove excess water, then marinate and sear for a crispy, golden crust. Tempeh, which has a nuttier flavor and firmer texture, is great crumbled into sauces, sliced into sandwiches, or stir-fried with veggies. Both are incredibly versatile and absorb marinades like a dream.

Edamame (young soybeans) are another great source of complete protein. A handful of steamed, salted edamame makes a perfect snack or salad topping. You can also blend them into dips or toss them into grain bowls for a pop of color and nutrition.

Whole grains like quinoa, farro, buckwheat, and bulgur might not be the first things that come to mind when you think of protein, but many are surprisingly protein-rich. Quinoa, in particular, is a complete protein, meaning it contains all nine essential amino acids. Use it as a base for bowls, stuff it into peppers, or add it to soups and salads to boost both heartiness and nutrition.

Nuts and seeds are small but mighty. Almonds, peanuts, cashews, sunflower seeds, chia, flax, and hemp seeds all offer good doses of protein along with healthy fats. Add them to smoothies, sprinkle them on oatmeal or yogurt, blend them into nut butters, or use them as a crunchy coating for roasted vegetables or tofu. Even better, nut and seed butters — like almond butter or tahini — are great in dressings, sauces, and baked goods.

Dairy and eggs round out the list for vegetarians. Greek yogurt, cottage cheese, and cheese offer high-quality protein and can be used in both savory and sweet dishes. Eggs, of course, are one of the most efficient and versatile protein sources out there — scrambled, poached, baked into frittatas, or boiled for a snack.

Combining these protein sources is key to building balanced, satisfying meals. Try pairing beans with grains (like rice and black beans), tofu with peanut sauce and brown rice, or a quinoa and chickpea salad topped with nuts and seeds. These combinations not only ensure you're getting enough protein but also bring exciting textures and flavors to the plate.

Going meatless doesn't mean sacrificing nourishment. With a pantry stocked with these plant-based options, you can fuel your body, satisfy your hunger, and get creative in the kitchen — all while enjoying meals that are just as hearty, delicious, and protein-packed as their meaty counterparts.

Dairy-Free Sauces & Substitutes

Whether you're lactose-intolerant, vegan, or simply cutting back on dairy, it's never been easier—or tastier—to explore dairy-free alternatives. Dairy-Free Sauces & Substitutes open the door to a world of creamy, flavorful, and satisfying options that can rival (and often outshine) their traditional dairy-based counterparts. From silky sauces to creamy spreads and cheesy toppings, these swaps allow you to enjoy your favorite meals while staying plant-based or dairy-conscious.

Let's start with one of the most beloved comfort foods: cheese sauces. While traditional cheese relies heavily on dairy, dairy-free versions use a clever combination of plant-based ingredients to mimic its creamy texture and umami flavor. Nutritional yeast is a star in this arena — its nutty, cheesy taste makes it ideal for vegan "cheese" sauces. Blend soaked cashews with nutritional yeast, garlic, lemon juice, a splash of plant-based milk, and a bit of mustard for a luscious, pourable sauce perfect for mac and cheese, nachos, or roasted vegetables.

Cashews are also a foundation for many dairy-free creams. Once soaked and blended, they turn incredibly smooth and rich, making them perfect for creamy pasta sauces, salad dressings, or even sweet desserts like cheesecakes and frostings. Add a pinch of salt and a squeeze of lemon, and you've got a neutral base that can go savory or sweet.

For those looking for a shortcut, store-bought dairy-free milks and creams have come a long way. Almond, oat, soy, and coconut milks can all be used in cooking depending on the dish. Oat milk has a naturally creamy texture and is great for béchamel or mashed potatoes, while full-fat coconut milk adds richness to curries, soups, and desserts. Dairy-free yogurt (especially coconut or almond-based varieties) can sub in for sour cream or be used in marinades, dips, and baking.

Plant-based butters and oils also play a key role in dairy-free cooking. Vegan butter can be used cup-for-cup in baking or cooking, and coconut oil gives a rich mouthfeel in frostings or crusts. Avocado, though unconventional, can even stand in for butter in baked goods or be mashed and used in creamy dressings.

For savory dishes, tahini, made from ground sesame seeds, is a versatile, dairy-free powerhouse. It's creamy, slightly bitter, and blends beautifully into sauces and dressings. Use it to make dairy-free Caesar dressing, lemon tahini sauce, or mix it with maple syrup for a sweet drizzle over fruit or baked goods.

And let's not forget dairy-free pesto — simply replace the Parmesan with nutritional yeast and use any combination of basil, spinach, arugula, or even carrot tops for a vibrant sauce. Blend it with olive oil, nuts (like pine nuts or cashews), garlic, and lemon juice for a fresh, zippy finish to pasta, roasted vegetables, or sandwiches.

Need something to replace cream cheese or ricotta? Whipped tofu, blended cashews, or almond-based cream cheese alternatives work beautifully in dips, spreads, and layered dishes like lasagna or baked ziti. Silken tofu, when blended with lemon juice and herbs, creates a light, tangy spread that's as versatile as it is protein-rich.

Ultimately, going dairy-free doesn't mean going without. These substitutes allow you to reimagine your favorite recipes, broaden your culinary creativity, and support dietary preferences without missing out on richness, flavor, or satisfaction. Whether you're experimenting or fully committed to a dairy-free lifestyle, these options make it easy to keep your meals creamy, dreamy, and completely plant-powered.

Creative Vegan Desserts

Vegan desserts have come a long way from the days of dry cookies and bland fruit cups. Today, they're just as decadent, beautiful, and satisfying as their dairy- and egg-laden counterparts—sometimes even more so. Creative Vegan Desserts celebrate the incredible possibilities that come with plant-based baking, proving that you can enjoy all your favorite treats without animal products, and with absolutely no compromise on flavor or texture.

At the heart of every good vegan dessert is smart substitution. Eggs, butter, and milk can all be swapped out with plant-based ingredients that not only perform beautifully in baking but often add their own unique health benefits and flavor dimensions. Flaxseeds or chia seeds mixed with water create a binding "egg" that's perfect for cookies, muffins, and brownies. Mashed bananas, applesauce, or pumpkin puree also work wonders for both texture and moisture, especially in cakes, quick breads, and pancakes.

For dairy-free richness, coconut milk, almond milk, oat milk, and cashew milk are staples that can seamlessly replace regular milk in everything from custards and puddings to frostings and ice creams. Coconut cream in particular is a dream ingredient—whip it up for a velvety topping or fold it into chilled cheesecakes and mousse for a decadent, creamy finish.

Let's talk indulgence. Vegan chocolate is now widely available and can be used to create silky ganache, fudgy brownies, or molten lava cakes that rival any traditional recipe. Date-based caramel made from blended dates, nut butter, vanilla, and a pinch of salt is a sticky-sweet, healthier twist on the classic that's perfect for layering in bars or drizzling over fruit. Add a handful of chopped nuts and dark chocolate chips to the mix and you've got a no-bake dessert bar that's gooey, crunchy, and completely irresistible.

Avocado-based chocolate mousse is another showstopper — smooth, rich, and lightly sweet, it's a dessert that's easy to make and packed with healthy fats. Sweeten it with maple syrup, blend with cocoa powder and a splash of vanilla, and chill for a dessert that tastes way more indulgent than it sounds.

When it comes to baked goods, vegan cakes, cookies, and cupcakes are now virtually indistinguishable from the traditional versions. Use plant-based milk with apple cider vinegar to create a buttermilk substitute that gives cakes a tender crumb. Vegan butter or refined coconut oil brings richness to frostings and doughs, while nut butters can enhance both flavor and structure.

And let's not forget fruit-based desserts. Roasted stone fruits with maple and cinnamon, baked apples stuffed with oats and raisins, or frozen banana "nice cream" blended with berries or cocoa powder — all are light, naturally sweet, and deeply satisfying. Top with crushed nuts, coconut flakes, or a spoonful of nut butter for a well-rounded treat.

The best part about creative vegan desserts? They invite experimentation. Without the constraints of traditional baking, you're free to explore new ingredients, flavors, and textures. Vegan baking is not just a diet-friendly alternative — it's a playground for creativity. From aquafaba meringues and tofu cheesecakes to almond flour brownies and cashew-based frosting, the possibilities are endlessly delicious.

So whether you're fully plant-based or just dessert-curious, these sweet treats prove that vegan desserts can be everything you want them to be: luscious, comforting, fun, and 100% satisfying — with zero compromise and plenty of heart.

Chapter 11
Feasts & Gatherings – Cooking for a Crowd

There's a special kind of magic that happens when people gather around a table. The laughter, the clinking of glasses, the stories shared between bites — food has a way of bringing everyone closer. In this chapter, we focus on recipes and strategies for feeding a crowd, whether it's a festive holiday dinner, a birthday bash, or a casual backyard get-together.

Cooking for many doesn't have to mean stress or chaos. With a bit of planning and the right recipes, you can serve up impressive dishes that look and taste amazing — without spending all day in the kitchen. From show-stopping mains and generous platters to easy starters and shareable sides, these dishes are built for abundance and flavor.

We'll also explore tips for prepping ahead, balancing your menu, and making meals that cater to a range of tastes and dietary needs. Think vibrant salads, hearty baked dishes, finger foods, and crowd-pleasing desserts — each one designed to keep things simple, delicious, and celebratory.

This chapter is all about the joy of sharing. Food becomes an experience when it's enjoyed together — a feast of not just flavors, but of connection and community. So set the table, turn up the music, and cook with love. Your guests will taste it in every bite.

Festive Appetizers & Starters

Every great gathering begins with anticipation — and nothing sets the tone like a well-crafted appetizer. Festive Appetizers & Starters are more than just nibbles before the main event; they're conversation starters, mood setters, and often the most memorable bites of the night. Whether you're hosting a holiday feast, a casual get-together, or an elegant dinner party, these small plates are your chance to impress without the stress.

Festive starters shine when they combine visual appeal, bold flavors, and just the right size for guests to enjoy in a bite or two. Think vibrant colors, varied textures, and surprising twists that make even familiar ingredients feel special. From delicate canapés to warm, cheesy dips, there's something truly joyful about sharing a table filled with little dishes that invite everyone to graze, savor, and linger.

Let's start with the classics reimagined. Miniature versions of familiar dishes always wow — think bite-sized caprese skewers with cherry tomatoes, mozzarella pearls, and basil leaves drizzled with balsamic glaze, or tiny puff pastry tartlets filled with caramelized onions and goat cheese. These make-ahead-friendly options pack a punch and look beautiful arranged on a platter.

Dips and spreads are a crowd favorite for a reason. From a vibrant beet hummus to creamy spinach artichoke dip served warm with toasted pita, these dishes encourage casual, communal eating. For a festive flair, try a whipped feta and roasted red pepper dip, or a three-layer Mediterranean spread with hummus, olives, and diced cucumbers. Serve with a mix of crunchy vegetables, crackers, or warm naan triangles to complete the experience.

Stuffed bites are another beloved category of starters that feel festive and thoughtful. Try stuffing mushrooms with herbed breadcrumbs and cashew cream, or sweet dates with almond butter or vegan cheese and finishing with a touch of smoked paprika. Mini bell peppers filled with quinoa salad or spiced chickpeas also make for a colorful, satisfying finger food that suits all dietary needs.

Crispy starters like arancini (fried risotto balls), tempura vegetables, or baked samosas offer texture and golden appeal. You can prepare these ahead of time and reheat just before serving — they're the kind of crispy-crunchy bites that vanish quickly, so make more than you think you'll need!

Want to go ultra-elegant? Try spoon or shot-glass appetizers like chilled cucumber soup, avocado mousse with roasted corn, or a dollop of beetroot puree with walnut pesto. These upscale bites are ideal for formal events and give a restaurant-quality touch to your home dining experience.

Festive doesn't have to mean complicated. Sometimes the most beloved appetizers are the simplest: a platter of marinated olives, roasted nuts with rosemary and sea salt, or crostini topped with smashed peas and lemon zest. A little seasonal garnish — fresh herbs, edible flowers, or citrus zest — can transform even the most basic starter into something that feels celebratory and intentional.

Finally, presentation is everything when it comes to appetizers. Use tiered trays, wooden boards, colorful ceramics, and fresh garnishes to create a visual feast that draws guests in. Mixing hot and cold options, creamy and crunchy textures, and familiar and unexpected flavors makes the experience exciting and welcoming.

So the next time you gather with friends or family, start strong with a spread of festive appetizers. These small but mighty dishes bring people together, spark joy, and build anticipation for the delicious meal to come — all while making your table look absolutely irresistible.

Shareable Mains & Platters

There's something deeply comforting and celebratory about placing a large dish in the center of the table, inviting everyone to dig in together. Shareable Mains & Platters bring back the magic of communal eating — where food becomes more than sustenance, and every dish becomes a conversation starter. Whether you're feeding family, entertaining guests, or enjoying a cozy gathering with friends, these generous, crowd-pleasing meals are made to be passed, served, and enjoyed in good company.

At the heart of every great shared meal is abundance — not in complexity, but in generosity. These are dishes that feel plentiful, colorful, and welcoming. Think roasted vegetable trays layered with herbs and grains, build-your-own taco spreads with vibrant toppings, or sizzling sheet pans of spiced tofu, grilled chicken, or baked fish surrounded by golden potatoes and fresh garnishes.

One of the most versatile ways to serve a group is with platter-style meals. Large wooden boards or trays filled with complementary ingredients create a feast for the eyes and the appetite. A Mediterranean mezze platter, for example, might include falafel, hummus, pita, olives, marinated vegetables, tabbouleh, and grilled halloumi. Everything can be prepped in advance and arranged beautifully just before serving — no last-minute stress required.

Baked casseroles and layered dishes are another perfect fit for sharing. Think baked ziti bubbling with sauce and melted cheese, a creamy vegan lasagna stacked with vegetables and tofu ricotta, or a big pan of enchiladas with plenty of toppings on the side. These dishes come out of the oven ready to serve, and they often taste even better the next day.

Family-style mains like paella, biryani, or a hearty rice pilaf packed with vegetables, spices, and nuts make for stunning centerpieces. They're fragrant, satisfying, and easy to scale for larger groups. A big pot of chili or stew — with crusty bread or cornbread on the side — also invites guests to serve themselves, customize their bowl, and come back for seconds.

For a more interactive experience, consider DIY-style platters that let everyone build their own meal. Taco bars, grain bowl stations, or wrap spreads with various fillings and sauces allow guests to tailor their plate to their tastes and dietary preferences. This style of eating is especially accommodating for mixed groups with vegetarians, gluten-free eaters, or picky palates.

Presentation plays a big role in shareable meals. Use big platters, rustic bowls, colorful linens, and lots of fresh herbs or citrus slices to make the table pop. Shareable meals are meant to feel festive and relaxed, so don't be afraid to go for big, bold displays. A beautiful platter piled high with grilled vegetables, dips, and warm bread is both nourishing and impressive — and it invites people to reach in, taste, and connect.

The best part about shareable mains? They encourage connection. Passing plates, serving one another, and enjoying a common dish builds a sense of togetherness that's harder to find in individually plated meals. It turns dinner into an experience — one where everyone lingers a little longer, laughs a little louder, and eats a little more than planned.

So whether you're hosting a feast or just want to make your weeknight meal feel special, lean into the joy of shared plates. With thoughtful preparation and a touch of creativity, Shareable Mains & Platters transform the act of eating into something memorable, nourishing, and full of heart.

Side Dishes to Impress

They may not be the main event, but the best side dishes have a special way of turning an ordinary meal into something unforgettable. Side Dishes to Impress are the kind that make your guests pause after the first bite — the kind that are every bit as carefully crafted as the entrée. Whether you're preparing a dinner party, a holiday feast, or simply elevating your everyday cooking, these sides offer a chance to get creative, go bold, and complement your meal with flair and flavor.

What makes a side dish truly impressive isn't complexity—it's balance and personality. The best ones offer contrast, enhance the main course, and bring their own unique charm to the table. They can be bright and refreshing, rich and comforting, crisp and crunchy, or silky and smooth. A well-chosen side dish doesn't just fill a plate—it completes it.

Take vegetables, for example. Roasting them with intention can elevate even the simplest produce. Charred Brussels sprouts with maple-balsamic glaze, caramelized carrots with cumin and honey, or roasted beets with orange zest and pistachios offer depth and complexity, while still letting the natural flavor of the vegetables shine. A sprinkle of fresh herbs, a drizzle of good olive oil, or a dusting of toasted nuts can take a basic roast to next-level territory.

Grain-based sides are another way to impress while keeping things hearty and elegant. A wild rice pilaf with dried cranberries, herbs, and toasted almonds brings nutty, chewy texture and beautiful color to any plate. Farro with roasted mushrooms and truffle oil, or couscous with lemon zest, mint, and pomegranate seeds, deliver the kind of subtle, sophisticated flavors that complement both meat and plant-based mains alike.

For something cool and refreshing, try reinventing a salad as a centerpiece-worthy side. Forget limp greens — go for shaved fennel and orange with olive oil, heirloom tomato and burrata with basil drizzle, or a cucumber and radish salad with sesame-ginger vinaigrette. These sides are not only visually stunning but provide a light and bright contrast to richer main dishes.

Potatoes, of course, deserve their own spotlight. A classic mashed potato is always welcome, but why not mix things up with garlic-infused smashed potatoes, crispy herb-roasted fingerlings, or a gratin of thinly sliced sweet potatoes with coconut milk and thyme? These variations feel comforting and familiar while offering a fresh twist that gets people talking.

And don't underestimate the power of a bread-based side. Homemade garlic knots, focaccia studded with rosemary and olives, or cornbread with jalapeño and cheddar can act as both an accompaniment and a statement piece. Served warm and fresh from the oven, bread sides bring people together — hands reaching across the table, sharing pieces, and soaking up sauces.

Plating and presentation also play a role in elevating side dishes. Use serving bowls and platters that show off the colors and textures, garnish with microgreens or edible flowers for a touch of elegance, and serve family-style to invite interaction and conversation.

In the end, impressive sides are about thoughtfulness — the care you put into pairing flavors, the surprise element that makes a classic feel new, or the little details that show you went the extra mile. They don't need to be fussy or over-the-top; they just need to bring joy and balance to the plate.

So the next time you're planning a meal, give your side dishes the attention they deserve. Because when done right, they don't just support the star — they are the star.

Sweet Celebrations

There's something truly magical about dessert when it's made for a celebration. Whether it's a towering cake for a birthday, a tray of frosted cookies at the holidays, or a platter of pastries for a baby shower or wedding, Sweet Celebrations are about more than sugar — they're about joy, memories, and the little moments that make life feel extraordinary. These desserts mark milestones, express love, and bring people together in the most delicious way possible.

At the heart of any sweet celebration is the desire to make something beautiful and meaningful. Sure, taste is key — but presentation, personalization, and the intention behind the dish are what truly make it unforgettable. And the great news? You don't have to be a professional baker to create something stunning. With the right recipes, a few thoughtful touches, and a dash of creativity, anyone can whip up show-stopping sweets worthy of any occasion.

Let's start with cakes, the undeniable centerpieces of most celebrations. A layered vanilla sponge with fresh berries and whipped cream is a timeless classic, while a decadent chocolate cake with ganache and edible gold flakes brings elegance to any event. Want something playful? Try a funfetti cake with colorful sprinkles inside and out, or a citrus cake with zesty glaze and candied peel. Even a single-tier cake can feel grand when topped with fresh flowers, piped rosettes, or a glittering topper.

If you're looking for something a bit more interactive, consider a dessert bar or buffet. A build-your-own cupcake station, DIY cookie decorating table, or ice cream sundae bar gives guests the chance to personalize their treats and adds a playful, memorable element to your gathering. Bonus: these options are great for accommodating various dietary preferences and keeping both kids and adults entertained.

For more refined celebrations, mini desserts are the perfect way to impress without overwhelming. Petite tarts filled with lemon curd or pastry cream, bite-sized brownies dusted with powdered sugar, or elegant chocolate-dipped strawberries are easy to serve and visually stunning. A well-arranged tray of mixed treats, from macarons to truffles to shortbread cookies, feels like a celebration all on its own.

And let's not forget about seasonal and cultural sweets — those timeless recipes passed down through families or tied to specific holidays. From sticky date pudding at Christmas to baklava during Eid, from sugar skull cookies on Día de los Muertos to almond biscotti at Italian weddings, these treats connect us to heritage and tradition while also creating new memories with every bite.

Presentation plays a big role in the celebration. Use cake stands, tiered trays, festive linens, or even a sprinkle of edible glitter or gold leaf to elevate the visual appeal. Think about colors that match the theme of your event and use fruits, flowers, or themed decorations to tie it all together.

What makes Sweet Celebrations truly special is the emotion baked in. The cookies made with your kids, the pie your grandmother taught you to make, the cake you spent hours perfecting for a friend's milestone — these desserts are more than recipes. They're gestures of love, creativity, and connection.

So the next time a special occasion rolls around — big or small — take it as an invitation to create something sweet and heartfelt. Because in the end, it's not just about sugar and flour. It's about joy, generosity, and celebrating life's moments, one delicious bite at a time.

Chapter 12
Tips, Variations & Your Culinary Space

As we close this flavorful journey, it's time to shift focus from the recipes themselves to the creative space behind them — your kitchen. This final chapter is a collection of practical tips, smart substitutions, and personal touches to help you grow as a confident, intuitive cook. After all, cooking isn't just about following instructions — it's about making each dish your own.

We'll begin with time-saving hacks, storage tips, and ideas for reducing food waste — because a well-organized kitchen is a happy kitchen. You'll learn how to store herbs to keep them fresh longer, repurpose leftovers into new meals, and master the art of batch cooking for busy weeks.

Then, we'll explore variations for many of the recipes you've already seen. Want to make a dish gluten-free, dairy-free, vegetarian, or lower in sodium? We've got you covered. You'll find ingredient swaps, flavor upgrades, and portion adjustments to match your dietary needs and taste preferences.

And finally, we've left a space just for you — your own recipe pages. Here you can jot down family favorites, new creations, or adjustments to the recipes you've tried. This isn't just a cookbook; it's a living, evolving part of your culinary life.

So keep experimenting, keep tasting, and most importantly — keep enjoying the process. Your kitchen is your canvas, and the recipes are just the beginning.

Ingredient Swaps & Smart Substitutions

Every cook has been there — halfway through a recipe only to realize you're missing a key ingredient. Or maybe you're cooking for someone with a dietary restriction, or simply want to make a healthier or more budget-friendly choice. That's where Ingredient Swaps & Smart Substitutions come in. With a little creativity and some tried-and-true alternatives, you can still whip up delicious, satisfying meals without running to the store or compromising on taste or texture.

Smart substitutions are more than just quick fixes — they're opportunities to customize dishes, make them your own, and even discover new favorite combinations. From baking essentials to cooking oils, from dairy to meat alternatives, swapping ingredients doesn't have to mean sacrificing flavor. In fact, it can often enhance it.

Let's start with baking basics. If you're out of eggs, try using a flax or chia egg (1 tablespoon ground flaxseed or chia seeds mixed with 3 tablespoons water). Mashed banana, applesauce, or pumpkin puree also work well in moist baked goods like muffins, pancakes, or brownies. For butter, coconut oil, vegan margarine, or even avocado can step in, while non-dairy milk like almond, soy, oat, or coconut milk easily replaces cow's milk in nearly every recipe.

Sugar swaps are another great way to adapt recipes for health or personal taste. Try using maple syrup, honey (for non-vegans), agave, or coconut sugar instead of white sugar. These alternatives not only offer a different flavor profile but often come with added nutrients and a lower glycemic index. Just remember that liquid sweeteners can alter the texture of baked goods, so you may need to slightly reduce other liquids in the recipe.

For savory dishes, missing ingredients can often be replaced with pantry staples. Out of tomato paste? Use tomato sauce or pureed canned tomatoes and simmer a little longer to thicken. No sour cream? Try Greek yogurt or a blend of yogurt and lemon juice for that tangy creaminess. If you're out of heavy cream, you can mix plant-based milk with a bit of olive oil or melted butter to replicate the fat content.

Gluten-free? Swap all-purpose flour with almond flour, oat flour, chickpea flour, or a store-bought gluten-free flour blend. These flours all behave differently, so some trial and error may be needed, but the results can be surprisingly delicious — often with more flavor and nutrients than standard white flour.

Dairy-free cooking is simpler than ever. Instead of cheese, use nutritional yeast for a cheesy flavor, or explore the many plant-based cheeses now available. Cashew cream, coconut milk, or soy-based products can create luscious sauces, soups, and desserts that are every bit as rich and satisfying as their dairy counterparts.

Trying to cut back on meat? Swap lentils or mushrooms for ground meat in tacos, pastas, and sauces. Tofu, tempeh, and jackfruit can stand in for everything from chicken to pulled pork. These alternatives are not only better for the environment — they also add fiber and other nutrients that meat can't match.

In the end, ingredient swaps are about confidence and flexibility. When you understand your ingredients — their purpose, texture, and flavor — you unlock the freedom to cook creatively, intuitively, and resourcefully. You no longer need to see missing items as deal-breakers, but as invitations to experiment.

So go ahead — embrace the unexpected, trust your instincts, and keep this list of smart substitutions close. Because with a little knowledge and imagination, any dish can be saved, transformed, or even improved.

Plating & Presentation Tips

We eat with our eyes first — and no matter how delicious a dish may be, thoughtful plating and presentation can make it feel even more special. Whether you're preparing a romantic dinner, hosting friends, or simply cooking for yourself, a beautifully plated dish adds a sense of care, artistry, and intention. Plating & Presentation Tips aren't just for fancy restaurants or Instagram — they're simple techniques anyone can use to elevate home cooking and make every meal feel like an occasion.

First, start with the plate itself. White or neutral-colored dishes are classic because they let the food's natural colors shine. But don't be afraid to mix things up — rustic ceramic plates or dark slate platters can add contrast and drama, especially for vibrant dishes like salads, pasta, or desserts. Choose a plate that fits the portion — too large, and the food can feel lost; too small, and it might seem crowded.

Next, consider the arrangement. Think in terms of balance, height, and space. Odd numbers are naturally pleasing to the eye, so if you're placing elements like meatballs, sliced fruit, or cookies, try grouping them in threes or fives. Play with height by stacking or layering ingredients — a mound of grain topped with roasted vegetables and garnished with herbs has more visual interest than if it were spread flat on the plate.

Leave a little negative space — don't feel the need to cover every inch of the plate. A clean, open area draws the eye to the food and gives your dish a modern, elegant look. You're not just serving a meal; you're framing it.

Color is your friend. Think of the plate as a palette and your ingredients as paint. Use contrasting colors for visual pop — bright herbs on creamy pasta, pomegranate seeds on hummus, or grilled carrots over a bed of greens. Add a pop of brightness with a lemon wedge, edible flower, or a streak of sauce — these details show attention and elevate even the simplest dish.

Garnishing is about more than looks — it should add flavor and texture, too. Fresh herbs like parsley, basil, or cilantro not only brighten a dish visually but also add a final layer of aroma and taste. Crushed nuts, a sprinkle of flaky sea salt, a few chili flakes, or a swirl of yogurt or pesto can completely transform the final look and mouthfeel.

Don't forget about sauces and drizzles. Instead of pouring sauce haphazardly, use a spoon, squeeze bottle, or brush to apply it artfully. A swoosh, dot pattern, or drizzle over the top can give a dish that "chef's kiss" presentation. Be intentional but not overly fussy — the goal is to enhance, not overwhelm.

For bowls and platters, layering and grouping is key. Build from the bottom up — grain, protein, veggies, then toppings. Use color blocking (placing different elements next to each other without mixing) to showcase the variety of ingredients, especially in salad or grain bowls. Platters can be styled with loose clusters and varying heights to look full and abundant without being messy.

Finally, take a step back before serving. Wipe off any drips or splashes around the rim of the plate, adjust any elements that shifted during plating, and give your dish a moment of appreciation. After all, food that's plated with love and intention tastes even better.

So whether you're plating tacos, tarts, or tofu, take a few extra minutes to make your food look as good as it tastes. Because presentation isn't about perfection — it's about making the moment feel special.

Storing, Freezing, and Reheating

Cooking is only half the battle — what happens after the meal matters just as much. Whether you're prepping ahead, saving leftovers, or batch-cooking for the week, knowing how to properly store, freeze, and reheat your food ensures that every bite stays safe, fresh, and flavorful. Storing, Freezing, and Reheating is a quiet skill that transforms your kitchen from a one-meal space into a time-saving, waste-reducing powerhouse. It's about making the most of what you make — and doing it with confidence.

Let's start with storing. Proper storage keeps food fresh longer and reduces the chance of spoilage. Always let hot food cool slightly before covering and refrigerating — placing piping hot food directly into the fridge can raise the temperature inside and affect other items. Use airtight containers to lock in moisture and flavor, and label everything with the date so you know how long it's been sitting.

When storing cooked meals or components, think in portions. Divide large batches into single servings so they're easier to grab-and-go later — whether for lunch, quick dinners, or snacks. Use clear containers so you can see what you have, and place older items toward the front of the fridge to remind yourself to use them first.

Freezing is your best friend when it comes to saving time and reducing waste. Not all dishes freeze well — creamy sauces may separate, and fried foods may lose their crispness — but many meals, like soups, stews, casseroles, baked goods, and cooked grains, freeze beautifully. Cool foods completely before freezing, and use freezer-safe containers or heavy-duty resealable bags with the air pressed out to prevent freezer burn.

Label each item clearly with the name and date. For extra organization, keep an inventory list on your freezer door. Frozen meals are best used within 2–3 months for peak flavor and texture, though many are safe to eat longer.

When freezing, consider separating certain components. For example, freeze pasta sauces separately from cooked noodles, or keep salad dressings apart from roasted vegetables. This way, textures are better preserved, and reheating becomes more flexible.

Reheating is more than just warming up — it's about bringing food back to life. For stovetop reheating, use gentle heat and add a splash of water, broth, or oil to loosen things up and prevent drying out. For the oven, cover casseroles or roasted items with foil to retain moisture. Set your oven to a moderate temperature (around 325–350°F or 160–175°C) and check frequently to avoid overcooking.

Microwaves are convenient, but they can be uneven. To get the best results, stir halfway through, cover the dish with a microwave-safe lid or wrap to trap steam, and use lower power settings to heat gradually rather than blasting on full power.

When reheating frozen meals, thawing overnight in the fridge helps preserve texture and ensures even heating. However, if you're short on time, many soups, stews, and grain dishes can go straight from freezer to pot — just heat slowly and stir often.

It's also helpful to know when not to reheat. Some foods — like delicate greens, crispy-fried items, or certain seafoods — are better enjoyed fresh or repurposed into new dishes rather than reheated directly.

Mastering storage, freezing, and reheating helps you cook smarter, waste less, and enjoy delicious meals without the daily stress of starting from scratch. With a few containers, some labels, and a little planning, your kitchen becomes not just a space for cooking — but a space that works for you long after the meal is done.

Recipe Pages for Your Own Creations

Every great cook has a signature touch — a pinch of this, a splash of that, a flavor pairing that just works. While following recipes is a wonderful way to learn and explore, the real magic happens when you start making dishes your own. *Recipe Pages for Your Own Creations* is your invitation to step into the role of recipe developer, flavor artist, and memory-maker. It's a space designed just for you — to document, adapt, and personalize your favorite culinary creations.

Perhaps it's the lemon tart you tweaked with lavender, or the chili you perfected with just the right amount of cocoa and spice. Maybe it's the smoothie blend that fuels your mornings or the pasta dish that always gets rave reviews from friends. These are the recipes that deserve to be remembered — not scribbled on scraps of paper or lost in a sea of bookmarks, but written with intention and pride.

Use these pages to record your favorite flavor combinations, note ingredient swaps that worked wonders, and capture those small details that make a big difference. Write down what worked and how you might do it differently next time. These notes become your personal cooking journal — a living, evolving reflection of your growth in the kitchen.

There's no right or wrong way to create a recipe. Start with inspiration — maybe it's a dish from this book, a memory from your childhood, a seasonal ingredient that caught your eye, or a craving you just had to satisfy. From there, think about what you want the dish to be: warming and cozy? Bright and fresh? Fast and easy? Decadent and indulgent?

Then, build the base. Choose your main ingredients — grains, proteins, vegetables, fruits — and start layering in flavor with herbs, spices, sauces, and textures. Think about balance: salty and sweet, soft and crunchy, rich and acidic. Don't be afraid to experiment. Some of the best discoveries come from unexpected pairings or happy accidents.

As you test and taste, trust your instincts. Pay attention to how the food looks, smells, feels, and of course, tastes. Cooking is part science, part intuition — and every time you step into the kitchen, you sharpen both.

You might also use these pages to record recipes passed down from loved ones or to create new traditions of your own. These can become gifts — not just for your taste buds, but for future generations who may one day cook from your notes, adding their own flourishes along the way.

Want to give your recipe structure? Include a title, ingredients list, prep and cook times, serving size, and step-by-step instructions. But also feel free to sketch, draw, or just jot down thoughts freestyle. Make these pages feel like *you* — because that's what will make them timeless.

The most important thing is to start writing. Whether you're capturing a perfected masterpiece or just logging an idea for later, this is your space to be bold, curious, and creative.

Because the best recipes don't just feed the body — they tell a story. And now, it's your turn to write it.

Conclusion

As we reach the final pages of this book, take a moment to look back at the journey you've just traveled — not just through recipes, but through stories, techniques, and the pure joy of creating something meaningful in your kitchen. From simple breakfasts that fuel your mornings to vibrant veggie mains, celebratory sweets, and shareable platters that bring people together, this book wasn't just about what to cook — it was about how and why we cook.

At its core, cooking is a deeply human act. It's nourishment, yes — but it's also comfort, connection, creativity, and love. Whether you were flipping pancakes for your family, crafting a solo bowl of soup on a rainy evening, or preparing a feast for a celebration, you were doing something profound: you were turning raw ingredients into something whole, beautiful, and sustaining. That's no small thing.

Throughout these chapters, you've explored the building blocks of a confident kitchen: knowing your tools, organizing your pantry, mastering prep and flavor foundations. You've learned how to make smart swaps, design balanced meals, and turn humble ingredients into standout dishes. You've cooked across continents — from the fragrant spices of Asia to the sun-drenched flavors of the Mediterranean and the bold, soulful bites of Latin America. And you've created desserts and snacks that feed not just the body, but the spirit.

But more than anything, I hope this book gave you permission to experiment.

Cooking is not about perfection. It's about practice — about showing up to the cutting board or the stovetop with curiosity, courage, and a sense of play. Mistakes will happen (burned onions, broken sauces, under-seasoned stews — we've all been there), but those mistakes are part of your growth. Every less-than-perfect dish teaches you something. Every successful one builds your confidence. Every meal, whether grand or humble, is a step toward mastery — not of technique alone, but of flavor, intention, and joy.

Remember, the best meals don't come from following a recipe to the letter. They come from trusting your taste. You are the final judge of your food. Listen to your senses — the sizzle of oil in a pan, the aroma of garlic just as it starts to color, the way lemon lifts a sauce or salt brings balance. Cooking is a conversation between you and your ingredients. And once you learn the language, you can create anything.

More importantly, food is not just about the plate — it's about the experience. A quick weeknight stir-fry can be just as special as a five-course meal, if made with care. A loaf of banana bread can say "I love you" more clearly than a thousand words. A table surrounded by people — laughing, tasting, reaching for seconds — becomes a place of connection, of community. These are the moments we remember.

As you begin to create and collect your own recipes — those you modify, reinvent, or completely make up — know that you're building something even greater: your culinary identity. These are the meals you'll become known for. The dishes your friends and family request again and again. The flavors that one day might be passed down, scribbled on recipe cards or stored in the memory of someone you love. These meals will carry a part of you in every bite.

So take what you've learned here and keep building. Keep exploring. Try something new each week. Revisit a favorite with a twist. Cook with what's fresh, what's on hand, or what simply sounds good that day. Keep your pantry stocked, your knives sharp, and your curiosity alive.

And most of all, don't just cook when it's convenient. Cook because it matters. Because it's grounding. Because it connects you to your senses, to the seasons, to your culture and heritage — or to someone else's. Cook because it brings joy. Cook because it allows you to create something from your hands that can be shared with your heart.

This book is only the beginning. Your kitchen is your canvas. You're the artist now. So go forth and cook boldly, season generously, and serve with love.

Here's to your culinary journey — may it be delicious, ever-evolving, and filled with flavor in every sense of the word.

Bon appétit.

www.ingramcontent.com/pod-product-compliance
Lightning Source LLC
LaVergne TN
LVHW061527070526
838199LV00009B/395